D0984308

Library of English Renaissance Literature

THOMAS MORE

SIR THOMAS MORE (1527)
From a Portrait by Hans Holbein in the Frick Collection
(Photograph Courtesy of the Frick Art Reference Library)

THOMAS MORE

BY

DANIEL SARGENT

Interfecistis, interfecistis, hominem
omnium Anglorum optimum.

REGINALD, CARDINAL POLE, 1535

BOOKS FOR LIBRARIES PRESS
FREEPORT, NEW YORK

First Published 1933
Reprinted 1970

STANDARD BOOK NUMBER:
8369-5406-8

LIBRARY OF CONGRESS CATALOG CARD NUMBER:
71-119963

PRINTED IN THE UNITED STATES OF AMERICA

TO

MY DAUGHTER

LOUISE ANNE SARGENT

CONTENTS

Chapter I

MORE'S EDUCATION

Thomas More was born in England fourteen hundred and seventy-eight years after the birth of Our Lord, and lived in this world more than two generations: fifty-seven years. Most of that time he spent in that great market-place, London, some of it at his King's court, and still less of it on the continent, in foreign countries, on diplomatic travel. But wherever he went during all those years, he was by all whom he met, remarked and remembered, for he had something very rare: a tongue both wonderfully witty and wonderfully friendly. That tongue of his made him known from Scotland to Hungary. In 1535, when he was fifty-seven he had his head taken off by the order of the King of England, Henry VIII, and from that time on he became equally widely known, not so much for his tongue as for his courage. But there was a quality in him deeper than either his courage or his wit, a quality which bore these other qualities: his shrewdness.

More had remarkable eyes. They could penetrate into a cause, into a man, and discern the good

from the bad. They made him an excellent judge:
an excellent judge in the specific sense, for he was
worthy to be what he became, the Lord Chancellor
of England; an excellent judge in all perplexities.
He could even measure the worth of his own
talents. He could see for what he was fitted. He
could see where his own affair ended, and another's
began. He, in a confusion of which most people
could make neither head nor tail, could perceive
wherein lay the real combat.

More's acumen was not only a talent which he
could use, it was a tendency which came near to
using him. It made him critical, almost satiric.
It bade him be suspicious of all enthusiasm, and
skeptical not only of his own spiritual exaltations,
but of those of others. When he had for half a
century judged well, he was asked by circumstances
to be judge as to whether or not he could take a
certain oath. That oath was one which he could not
see how in good conscience he could take. Yet if he
refused it he would be executed, as a traitor to his
king, and as a martyr to God. Traitor he knew he
was not. Martyr he was not worthy to be. So he
sought every way to avoid being presented with
the oath. Finally when a decision was demanded of
him, he the judge, gave it, going to his execution,
letting God make of him what he would, and careful only to be what he had always been, Thomas
More, Christian, and Londoner.

More learned this habit of looking at things twice from the people with whom he was brought up, and among whom he was to the end most at home, — the Londoners: merchants, lawyers, artisans. They were city people who lived by give and take, who calculated, who had to calculate. They were not materialists, for they had a fixed religious faith which vouched for the existence and importance of things spiritual. They had an eye out to their souls. But in everything they were bargaining, and not Quixotic. They left their money to the Church, when they could use it no more, — in their wills. But they left it. And they had a shrewdness about leaving it to the most pious priests who could best pray for the repose of their souls: the Franciscans. Not least sagacious of these Londoners was his father, John More.

More's father leaned over the cradle of his third-born child, and first-born son, and dedicated him to the only profession which he knew: that of lawyer; and to the only wisdom which he knew: that of London common-sense. The father's name was John More. He was a lawyer, the son of a lawyer, of a family which had risen in status through living two generations in London, but which, previous to that, had lain in such full obscurity that those addicted to genealogy can without any fear of being molested by evidence, argue endlessly as to whether that family's origin was English or Irish. He was but a young man still, twenty-six, yet he had gone some way on the road to success, and the times in which he lived had the privilege of giving a man more experience than he bargained for: they were days of civil war, of insecurity for citizens, of jeopardy for kings. Such a man could very well be, as his son was to be, skeptical of fortune, and not always sure that right would have might, yet he was in body the shape of a hearty confident man, and he had an imperturbable face which Holbein could paint a half a century later as still smiling. John More was the man who said that a man about to marry has about as much chance of choosing a good wife as a blind man has of dragging out of a bag which contains seven snakes to one eel, an eel. He was also the man who, listening to that own saying of his, married merrily three times. He played the part to that son of his, of not only a father, but a mother, — for the mother died, — and also of one or more elder brothers. He was, when More was two feet high, the giant of the world to his son, and the oracle of oracles. There was never any cleavage between John More and his son Thomas More. The sayings of the one continued to be spoken by the other.

The next great giant in More's life was Cardinal Morton. Says More of him: "He was of a mean stature, and though stricken in age, yet bore he his body upright. In his face did shine such an amiable reverence, as was pleasant to behold: gentle in communication, yet earnest and sage. He had great delight many times with rough speech to his suitors to prove, but without harm, what prompt wit and what bold spirit were in every man."

Cardinal Morton had experienced a life which teaches a special kind of wisdom, which I will not call a sense of expediency, but rather a sense of what is possible. He had begun his career in the Church in the days of the Lancastrian Kings, and when there came to be a fight for the throne between the Yorkists and the Lancastrians, he had held loyal to the Lancastrians, even to the extent of going into exile. But he had seen that it was no use to be stubbornly proud. When the Yorkists were definitely in power he had humbled himself, submitted to Edward IV, and keeping himself out of politics had risen in the Church to be Bishop of Ely. Then he had seen the death of Edward IV, and then the death by murder of Edward's little son, and a King Richard III on the throne whom he did not trust, and who did not trust him. And finally thrown into prison, and escaped from prison, he had conspired to elevate to the throne a new King, Henry VII, the best in sight under the circumstances. — He had seen much trouble.

He had seen much bloodshed and he wanted peace, and he was growing old. Above all, in

England there must be a strong king to end civil wars, and such a king had to be made out of the king at hand whether that king was naturally strong or not. The king at hand was indeed not strong. He had neither a kingly manner, nor kingly blood. He was Henry Tudor who had no more right of blood to the throne than his great-grandfather had, who was but the bastard of a man who might have been king if he had been older than his brothers. He had little prowess, and no great brain. But with due pageantry he might show for a king. And he had what was important for the moment, even in a king, unkingly caution — which bordered on trickiness. — And if he had to have a vice, he had a vice that was convenient for the strengthening of his power, avarice. He was willing moreover to rely on men with clever brains, rather than on the nobles. And among those men who put astuteness into Henry's administration was the very same Bishop of Ely, John Morton. Henry was glad to have such a man to help him, made him Lord Chancellor of the realm, and had him created by the Pope Archbishop of Canterbury, and then Cardinal. Morton was glad to spend devotedly the last efforts of his life in making Henry VII a king, and his reign a reign.

How it came to pass that young Thomas More, son of a London lawyer, came to know and to learn from this foremost man of the realm was this way. The boy More had been sent at the age of seven to study under Nicholas Holt, an enthusiastic Latin grammarian and rhetorician, at St. Anthony's School, London, then the foremost school of the town. More did well in his studies. Holt knew Cardinal Morton and could recommend the boy. And More's father was growing important as a lawyer, and wished to have him so recommended. The Cardinal was glad always to accept young men of promise into his household. So Thomas More was sent to the Cardinal's palace at Lambeth there to learn — after the custom of a time less bookish than ours — how to be great by being apprenticed to greatness. More, before he was in his teens, was playing the part of page in a great man's household.

The schooling the boy got there was largely derived from keeping his eyes and ears open to what was going on. The court was frequented somewhat by scholars, and a great deal by statesmen and foreign ambassadors. The conversation at Morton's table was of great interest, and liveliness, and was filled with controversy over which Morton presided with good humor, and tolerance, as is described by More in the first book of the Utopia. It was a place of many opinions, but where those of the laconic and pithy Cardinal dominated.

More learned one thing definitely from the

Cardinal, not to trust fortune, not to be too proud when you were lifted on high, not to become heavy-hearted when you fell into disappointment and adversity. This bit of wisdom was taught not merely in maxims which everyone knew, nor by the words of the Cardinals, but, more important, by his actions. He had spent too much of his life in frustration, he had been disappointed too many times, now to be arrogant, or over-proud, or even over-confident, in his new honors. They were late honors. He was nearing three score years and ten. He had grown wise before he had been elevated to high place.

More learned another thing from the Cardinal — if he had not already learned it from his father: to mind one's own affairs. Particularly do not meddle with the quarrels of kings. Let the princes act on their platform as a pageant. Watch them. Do not climb to the platform and try to be one of the actors yourself, or you will suffer for your pains either from one or from both parties. Morton knew what he was talking about when he gave this counsel, and he could illustrate the counsel with anecdotes of his own experience, some of which the boy who listened to him, — Thomas More, — incorporated into his "History of Richard III", a book which contained so much of Morton's wisdom that scholars at one time ascribed the book to Morton, himself.

Morton told for instance of how he had tried to keep out of the quarrels of Kings when Richard III was usurper and reigning, and of how difficult had been his task. The usurper had tried to force Morton to declare himself as either for or against him, and had sent a friend to invite Morton to commit himself. Morton had refused. His reply had been as follows: "In good faith, my lord, I love not much to talk much of Princes, as thing not all out of peril, though the word be without fault, forasmuch as it shall not be taken as the party meant it, but as it pleaseth the Prince to construe it. And ever I think on Aesop's tale, that when the lion had proclaimed that on pain of death there should none horned beast abide in that wood, one that had in his forehead a bunch of flesh fled away a great pace. The fox, that saw him run so fast, asked him whither he made all that haste; and he answered, 'In faith, I neither wot nor reck, so were I once hence because of this proclamation made of horned beasts.' 'What, fool,' quoth the fox, 'thou mayest abide well enough; the lion meant not by thee, for it is none horn that is in thine head.' 'No, marry', quoth he, 'that wot I well enough. But what an he call it an horn, where am I then?'"

Not all the men at the Cardinal's palace at Lambeth were of Morton's ironic nature. There was there Henry Medwall, chaplain, who had a taste for Italian romantic comedy, and wished to

introduce its prettiness into England. He wrote
plays, in the nature of interludes and noble dialogues, which were acted by the pages of the
Cardinal, who inserted into them their London
realism. More's happy intrusion into these plays
has been described by William Roper, More's
son-in-law: "Yet would he at Christmas-tide
suddenly step in among the players, and never
studying for the matter, make a part of his
own there presently among them, which made
the lookers on more sport than all the players
beside."

Cardinal Morton, who by his life of disappoint-
ments was not eager to believe that every boy with
spirit would become a great man, prophesied great
things for this young intruder into plays. One day
when the Cardinal was seated at his table sur-
rounded by notables, he remarked of him: "This
child waiting at the table, whosoever shall live to
see it, will prove a marvellous man." But at the
same time the Cardinal did not want to spoil the
child by letting him become too important, too
much a favorite, at Lambeth. He sent him therefore at fourteen to Oxford University, to Canterbury Hall.

The voyage of Thomas More toward Oxford
must not be thought of as one toward medieval
towers and romance. It was a voyage towards a
country which was perhaps the most hard-headed

that ever existed: the country of the medieval intellect, the intellect of Christendom.

Oxford University was then, as it is now, an English school of learning on an English country-side, two days' walking distance west from London, but it was also a metropolis in a realm which cut across the national boundaries of Europe, and which was composed of some eighty universities scattered throughout Christendom. The citizens of this land, whatever their race, were fellow-citizens in a great commonwealth, and what they learned in their land, and what they taught in their land was never, — to their boast — local, but universal. They were clear-headed men, practised in disputation, and merciless in their logic. In such a land — I still call it a land, so real was it — mists that existed in adjoining regions disappeared. Fairy-tales could not enter it. Enthusiasms found themselves there sorely chastened. Precipitancy was rebuked.

As the great free country of the intellect was to the medieval mind a real country, so the scheme of studies in that country were real, founded on reality, real as a landscape. It was so fixed and so logical that it existed as the scheme of a tennis court exists to a tennis player, who knows that a tennis court will be the same, no matter where it will be, no matter whether it is planted round with lilacs or forsythia, or is made of this or that-colored clay. So clear was the scheme that it lent itself to be depicted even in design. It was a castle, outside of which stood shacks and pavilions, invitations to idleness. Inside its walls were seven noble flights of steps, up which a man who had grown ashamed of his ignorance, and who had resisted allurements could climb. Those flights of stairs were the Seven Liberal Arts: Grammar, Rhetoric, Dialectic, and then Arithmetic, Geometry, Music, Astronomy. They led him to become a Bachelor of Arts. Then he could proceed even farther, climbing to a higher terrace, becoming a philosopher, and then to a still higher terrace becoming a theologian. To him as a theologian belonged a turret at the castle's summit into which he could climb, and under the open sky, God's very sunlight, play the contemplative. Nothing in that castle was purposeless.

Merely to enter such a scheme of studies was a discipline. The plan of the castle reminded its inhabitant that he was more than an individual, more than an Englishman or a Frenchman: he was an intellectual man, whose personal or national peculiarities were not the measure of all things, and whose place of final halting had not the temporary marks of the villages to which he was used. Its divisions taught a man to be respectful not only of men of other nations, and other temperaments, but to do honor to those who were studying on other terraces. Its insistence on a scale of studies kept

the beginner from thinking that he knew everything, or that he was expected to know everything.
The logic of the castle preached humility, and advised a certain reserve to every man in the credence
which he was always ready to give to the suggestions of his fantasy.

More went to Oxford, probably in the year in
which Columbus discovered America, and spent
two years in the castle of learning, with which he
was already familiar. The general effect of the
sojourn was to make him even more level-headed
than before. He not only inhabited the castle, he
worked in it. He had to work, he says, for he had
nothing else to do, pleasures being denied him by
the foresight of his father who gave him but small
allowance, for which he thanks his father: "Thus
it came to pass that I indulged in no vice or vain
pleasure, that I did not spend my time in dangerous
or idle pastimes, that I did not even know the
meaning of extravagance and luxury, that I did
not learn to put money to evil uses, that in fine, I
had no love, or even thought, of anything beyond
my studies." His chief studies were rhetoric and
dialectic. He learned, particularly from the latter
study, to consider a truth not in its isolation, but
in relation to other truths. And through practise
in disputation, and through listening to disputation, he acquired that prudent habit of the scholastic thinkers: the marshalling of all objections to

your view, before you state your own view. There
was at Oxford but one thing which tended to make
him lose his head. That was the Greek enthusiasm.

The medieval curriculum had been designed not
by poets but by men with a scientific bent, the
metaphysicians, "the Schoolmen." In their curriculum they had given a place to the study of
poetry and rhetoric, — a proper place — but it
was not a place which those who liked eloquence,
thought worthy of them. They chafed at their
subserviency, yet could not rebel. They would
never have been able to rebel if the metaphysicians
had not thrown away their supremacy. They threw
it away by betraying their own cause, by losing
faith in their own logic, by using their disputations
for a purpose which belonged more properly to
rhetoricians — display. All of which gave the
rhetoricians a chance to organize a revolution
which they were in fact now beginning. Their great
battle-cry in that revolution was the word "Greek."

To shout such a battle-cry did not mean that
the shouter knew Greek, nor that he even intended
to learn Greek. It meant that he had been caught
by an enthusiasm which was ready to drag him,
if he did not look out, into absurdities far greater
than any he attacked. It would begin by asking
him to admire everything that was elegant and
gracious, and with the same breath to revile the
scholastic logicians, with their crabbed Latin and

syllogisms, as dunces and barbarians. Then to keep
the scholastic philosophers from answering back,
it could be denied that they were philosophers at
all. Philosophers were men who wrote sublimely,
like Plato, and men who did not write with that
grandeur were not philosophers. They were hair-
splitters and should be chased from the castle of
learning. Their lodgings in the castle should even
be demolished, and what had once been a towering
Gothic building should be transformed into a
Greek temple. The enthusiasm for Greek went to
lengths to which it never originally intended to go.
All real importance was taken away from philosophy, and the devotion which had once been accorded to holy Christian things was transferred to
pagan things. A vigil light in Italy was burned
night and day before a volume of Homer's Iliad.

The Greek enthusiasm had recently arrived at
Oxford, and it was, certainly as yet, scarcely at all
absurd there. It had been brought there by well-
balanced pious men, whose enthusiasm for Greek
was a sane enthusiasm for the wonders in that
language. Grocyn was at this time its great
teacher, and he was a great man as well by his
learning in Greek as by his humility. He had
simply introduced Greek into its due place in the
study of Grammar and of Rhetoric, in which it had
theoretically always been installed. Therefore, at
Oxford, Greek showed at its best, and could not

help but attract a young man like More who had a love of letters, and a practical man's repulsion to the excessive subtlety and even futility that had fallen on scholastic dialectics.

More became a Grecian. Not one of the hot-headed, light-headed kind, who thought that if they learned Greek they need no longer bother with logic. Not one of those, even more ridiculous, who thought they did not have really to learn Greek, — only to cheer for it. Not one of those whose confused minds treated philosophy as if it were something you ravishingly performed with, as with a flute. More was genuinely enthusiastic for the beauties of a language which deserved enthusiasm. He studied Greek grammar. He made himself a friend and disciple of Grocyn's. He so shone in the imitation of classic eloquence that he became the model Grecian to the other disciples of Grocyn. He was just about to take his place in the international circle of humanists, when his father stepped in, and summoned him from Oxford and from this dabbling with words, back to London, there to devote himself to the study of good sound English Common Law at the very English Inns of Court.

No man knows exactly how the London Inns of Court began, but every man knows they have been quite as important as the English Channel in making England England. Their solidarity, their sense of tradition, their tenacity, have preserved for England its English Common Law which distinguishes it from the Continent. The Common Law has been described as a "jumble," or by those who like it better as a "tough thicket." It has resisted good things and bad things: progress, logic, as well as tyrannizing kings. It has helped the English to resist the temptation of any absolutism, and to continue in their path of compromise, make-shift and precedent. Common law has at the bottom of it a profound skepticism. And its skepticism had its fortress in the Inns of Court whither More was now called. To its barristers the law schools of Oxford, whether of canon or civil law, were alike academic and visionary. Oxford thought about logic, London about precedent.

More began by entering an Inn of Chancery, New Inn, but that was merely a vestibule to Lincoln's Inn into which he was admitted on the Feast of the Purification, 1496, at the age of eighteen. His grandfather had begun by being a so-called butler at that Inn, which meant that the grandfather did all the secretarial writing for the society, kept the pension roll and the treasurer's roll, catalogued the library, and checked the students who spoke "too loud or too high in the hall," but was not a member of the Inn. So faithfully, however, had he performed his duties that he had been elected to the society. Thomas More was now elected to that same society, as one might be to a club, on the nomination of his father, who was one of its advanced members: its rulers, the benchers. Beneath the benchers were the barristers. Beneath the barristers were the clerks. Thomas More was a clerk. He had his oath to take and his dues to pay. Lincoln's Inn was a society in which one studied, and up through which one climbed as in Oxford's castle of learning. Automatically when a bencher became judge, he would be promoted to a different inn.

The legal training at Lincoln's Inn was not a course in theory. The student, the clerk, had to make himself acquainted with all the lack of logic in English common law, which was a thing incommunicable, and not to be grasped except by practice. Much of the training was done by the arguing of imaginary cases, but there were lectures also, which the distinguished benchers were required to give, but for which they received a fee, — £14 for the Lent term. It was, as this very requirement of the lectures from the benchers shows, a closely organized society in which there were as many privileges as obligations, and as many obligations as privileges, and with very little of that freedom in its modern sense of irresponsibility. Revels, for instance, were surely not a task; they were an hilarity which several times More, by being their elected marshal or leader, made more hilarious, yet a member of the Inn could be fined for not attending them. The Inns of Court had also their religious ceremonies and good works. They gave a formation to the whole of a man, put a stamp upon his whole personality.

More took the stamp of Lincoln's Inn. He revelled and studied with his fellow-clerks, and what we think was remarkable in his individuality led him only to be more affable and quick-witted than his companions, and thus to become more intimate with them and loved by them. He did not stand aloof, and was never for one instant looked at by them as a pedantic outsider. In later years he was to be chosen by them, more often than was usual, their lecturer or reader. He was to serve them as keeper of their "Black Book" of records, and to show his loyalty to them by lending their Inn at one time money. It was in 1496 that he had joined Lincoln's Inn. At the end of five years, in 1501, he was admitted to the Bar. He was then twenty-three, able to support himself and guide himself.

Chapter II

MORE'S CALLING

According to Erasmus, More had entered the Inns of Court only at the command of his father and against his own inclinations. Such was a statement which the disposition of Erasmus liked to make, and which it was very ready to believe true, for Erasmus found pleasure in thinking all good men were unhappy like himself, and it was incredible to him that any sane man could want to be a lawyer. More was to him eminently sane, and therefore must have been forced into the law. After he had entered the law he was to Erasmus like someone imprisoned. No, worse than that, he was like one of the victims whom Red Indians bind naked under mosquitoes. He was being tormented by the trivial cares of daily life, when he might have inhabited the delicious Elysium of the humanists, — in which place, of course, Erasmus himself was so perpetually restless.

More may have felt a qualm at leaving Grocyn, the Greek teacher, and at departing from the admiration which he had awakened for himself amid a small group at Oxford. He may have felt an

aversion for the law more deep than the mere dislike of any healthy man for hard work. That he
inherited no idolatry of the law from his father is
evident in the willingness with which, like all
humanists, he was ready to satirize lawyers, and
in the decisive fashion in which he exiled lawyers
as an absurdity from his reasonable commonwealth of Utopia. But More was not a romantic
poet being forced, melancholy, into a career which
he detested. There is no indication that he set up
any counter-suggestion to his father's projects of
making him another John More. More was a
realist. If he were not to become a lawyer, what
could he become? Suppose he had an aptitude for
letters, where was the position or pension for men
who followed letters as a profession? To become a
priest, and as a priest to be awarded a benefice,
was one way in which a man could devote himself
with some independence to polite literature at this
time, but More had too much respect for the
priesthood to be willing to become a priest for any
such unpriestly reason.

More entered the Inns of Court without hesitation, and his alacrity was especially admirable, for
he had no enthusiasm to drive him on, and he did
have talents which tended to make him delay. He
had an ability to imitate the Latin historians,
which led him later on to write a fragment of terse
and eloquent English history — "The History of

Richard III" — and which might have led him
to consider himself as a misunderstood, unappre-
ciated Tacitus.

He was also a poet, not like Spenser and Chaucer
who were so much greater as poets than as men —
but nevertheless a poet. There was always a part
of More which did not show in his verses, but
enough of him showed to make his verses recog-
nizable as his. Unlike absolutely worthless poetry
they have an individual mark, a combination of
cheerfulness and irony. He was enough of a poet
to write in the very real last days of his life, in the
Tower, while waiting for death, at least two poems.
You can hear the pathos, of which I speak, in such
of their lines as these:

"Long was I, Lady Luck! your Serving Man;
    And now have lost again all that I got."

He had certainly enough poetical talent in him
to find it wearisome labor poring over statutes,
and decisions.

More's most remarkable literary talent was
dramatic: an ability to invent dialogue. With that
ability he had stepped into the plays of Henry
Medwall. With that ability he was later to illustrate his controversial writings, and make his
conversation as good as a play. With that ability
he might, if he had lived a hundred years later,
have contributed to Elizabethan comedy. It was

a talent which must have made him a lover of leisure.

And finally, somewhat aside from this, he had, if not a taste for exact scholarship in languages, an extraordinary comprehension of tongues. Said Richard Pace, a statesman humanist, one of his Grecian friends: "Here I will remark that no one ever lived who did not first ascertain the meaning of words, and from them gather the meaning of sentences which they compose — no one, I say, with one single exception, and that is our own Thomas More. For he is wont to gather the force of the words from the sentences in which they occur, especially in his study and translation of Greek. This is not contrary to grammar, but above it, and an instinct of genius. Indeed, his genius is more than human, and his learning not only eminent, but so various that there is nothing of which he seems to be ignorant. His eloquence is incomparable and twofold, for he speaks with the same facility in Latin as in his own language. His sense of fun is joined with perfect refinement — you may call humor his father, and wit his mother."

More had no temptation to become a school-master, a grammarian, like his school-master Holt, but he did have a temptation to play with the artificial rhetoric of the humanists, to write letters like Cicero, to receive similar letters, and to bask in the mutual admiration which the humanists accorded to one another, and on which they lived.

More took his literary talents for exactly what they were worth. He put them in their place with his ever-ready irony, which he always preferred to direct against himself rather than against his friends. He did not suppress them. He used them. He used them to help him in his work, and he used them for amusement. His father — whom Erasmus paints so stern, — was proud of them. He was becoming a prosperous lawyer, and for a new house which he had bought, and a new wife whom he had married, he ordered some painted tapestries. He invited his son Thomas to compose the verses to go over these tapestries. Here is one of the legends, printed in old spelling in order that it may be, as it was, a decoration.

> "Old Age am I, with lokkes, thynne and hore,
>   Of our short lyfe, the last and best part.
>   Wyse and discrete, the publike wele therefore
>   I help to rule to my labor and smart.
>   Therefore Cupyde withdrawe thy fyry dart.
>   Chargeable matters shall of love oppresse
>   The childish game and ydle bysinesse."

And here is another verse which he wrote while a student of the law, concerning that subject which the turmoil of the day made people so acquainted with. And also it has a further interest for its unconscious prophecy. Let it be printed in modern spelling so that it can be nearer to our modern comprehension: (The *she* in it refers to the fickle lady, Fortune.)

"She suddenly enhanceth them aloft
And suddenly mischieveth all the flock.
The head that late lay easily and full soft
Instead of pillows lieth after on the block,
And yet, alas — the most cruel proud mock —
The dainty mouth that ladies kissed have,
She bringeth in the case to kiss a knave."

He also had time to continue his association with Grocyn who was now in London, and to pursue his Greek studies. With his comrades in the Greek enthusiasm, he competed in feats of classical dexterity. He wrote Latin verses for a school-boys' first reader. He wrote Latin epigrams for the admiration of mature Latinists. He translated the Greek Anthology, with the help of his friend Lilly, into Latin. He lectured on a masterpiece of Latin literature: "The City of God," by Saint Augustine. In these ways he gained for himself a lofty seat in that small but international circle of humanists, who like a group of Olympian Gods sat in their fancied peace above the Europe of their day. He disarmed their jealousy by his friendliness. He aroused their admiration by being different from them in his vivacity. He was the one humanist of whom the other humanists were not jealous.

More, if it had been but for his literary talents, would have been quite happy in the law. The only thing that disturbed him, and gave him misgivings during those first years at Lincoln's Inn, was of a quite different nature. It was a sense of the futility of any worldly profession in comparison with what would be his occupation forever and ever in the next world. With his penetrating eyes he had when very young pierced through the pageantry of success and failure which went on about him, and seen how temporary, if brilliant, it all was, and then for the easing of his heart, which had a tremendous longing for lasting companionship, he had been permitted by God to catch a glimpse of the eternal place, heaven. Once a man has caught such a glimpse, can he rightfully and happily continue in an occupation so mundane and self-important as that of the law? Might not that glimpse of heaven disappear if he gave himself too much to the law, and gained a success in the law? Did not the fact that he had received such a glimpse of the next world mean that God expected him to become a monk? Had not Our Lord called him to a special life of abandonment of the world? More was in a state of doubt which must have been painful, and which must have tempted him to make a precipitate decision in one sense or the other.

It was typical of More that in this difficulty he should have done nothing rashly, and should have distrusted his spiritual promptings as possibly coming from his mere sensibilities. Instead of entering some penitential order, he tried to live as sanely as possible in this world by keeping ironically in mind that death was ever at his elbow. This showed no great originality on his part, for such a practise was the favorite spiritual panacea of the time. Somehow or other men ran to that cure-all in an age of gold and finery and pageantry, and divinized kingship, as they have no need to do now-a-days, and had no need to do in the age of catacombs. It made them not melancholy, but merry. More lived at a time when the famous Dance of Death was still but freshly painted in the Cloister of Saint Paul's Cathedral. Poetry, painting, pageant were filled with that same dancing skeleton.

And aside from that, the reality of death was very dramatically before men. In the very first year when Henry VII came to the throne there broke out in England a plague which recurred at intervals, and inserted its terrors into the political history of the next fifty years. It was a very deadly plague called the "sweating sickness," killing off in 1498 in London alone thirty thousand people. It slew a few years later More's patron, Cardinal Morton. In appearance the plague was very sensational. Says the Chronicler of its first appearance: "In this year a new sickness did reign, and is so sore and painful as never was suffered before, the which was called the burning sweat. And this was so intolerable, that men could not keep their beds; but as lunatic persons, and out of their wits, ran about naked, so that none almost escaped that were infected therewith." — It was not very difficult to remember death.

Death helped a man to value earthly success for what it was worth, and took away from him a false sense of security. It also made him not afraid of anything that man can do. In the year 1499 there took place in London a nauseating execution. It was that of a young man, Warwick, of much more royal blood than the King himself, who had been kept in the Tower, and had lately been deliberately incriminated in a rebellion. He was not a winning young man. He had been kept too long in the tower, like a worm white in a cellar. Yet it was sickening to have him tricked, and then retricked into confessing his crimes, and then to have him publicly disembowelled, and then cut up into four equal parts. People shook their heads. — "Beware of Kings." — More taught himself to beware of kings not at all. He used to remark that we are all of us at any rate prisoners condemned to death. We are all riding in a cart to execution, some of us to an execution a little farther off than the others.

Why bother about what kings can give or about what kings can take away? Keep your mind on important things.

More liked to taste that good "treacle" — he called it — the thought of death. It made a man of him, a good companion, not a proud pedant. But was any mere thought enough? Might he not become beguiled by flattery, or spoiled by high place? He seriously considered hiding himself from the world's applause and reward.

Half a thousand years before this, about the time when William, the Conqueror, was winning fame by conquering England, there was another man in Europe who was fleeing from fame, who had the same apprehension of success which touched the heart of Thomas More. Born in the Rhineland, this man had also been a lawyer, — though a priest, — a canon lawyer, and teacher at Rheims, the city of the French kings. So brilliant was he that he could not escape advancement in the Church, and came to be named Archbishop of Rheims, at which he fled to be forgotten, first to a Benedictine Monastery, — but there he might be known and praised, — and then southward until from a saintly bishop of Grenoble where the Alps and a wilderness began, he begged a safe retreat, he and his few companions. Hence in heaven the name, the fame, the soul of this man, Saint Bruno. Hence on earth his foundation, the Carthusian

Order, that order of all orders which is perhaps
most separated from this earth, for whereas members of other orders are at least after their death
known with the title saint before them, who is it
that knows the Carthusian saints? They are truly
not for our eyes. They are as nearly white and elect
in heaven as living men can be. Their art of singing
is artless in a way which we should not try on earth
to follow. Their record, that of an order which
during a thousand years has not needed reform, is
not such a record as this world allows or expects.
Hence, — I say, — the Carthusian Order. Hence
La Grande Chartreuse. Hence the great fleet of
motor lorries which carry as if for a drive in a war
the gaping tourists on summer days to stare at
that huge edifice of inviolable quiet which the
French Government has deprived of that even
greater silence of the monks. Hence our — before
their lives — ineffable incomprehension.

There was at the time of More a house of the
Carthusians in London. A crusader had established
it there, and because most of the Carthusian
houses are in the forests and fields, this one which
became more and more swallowed up by the city,
took on a special individuality. It became a part
of the city, and even if its inmates could be dis-
persed by the tyranny of the Renaissance, its name
could never be eradicated: Charterhouse. One of the
peculiarities of the Carthusian house in London

was that on its property there were houses in which could be lodged unmarried men who were not of the order. More while studying at Lincoln's Inn, lived for four years with the Carthusians, (probably in one of these houses), following in as far as was possible for the law student, their prayers, their austerities, but without vows.

Was he intended by God to stay in that Charter-house, to become a part of it? The house itself was an inspiration by its austerity, its heavenliness. According to a monk-hater (Froude), had all monks been like those of the Charterhouse, there would have been no "Reformation", nor any need of a "Reformation". But living as the Carthusians live, each monk so shut off from his fellow-monks, might not be appropriate to More's disposition, for he was eminently sociable. He might elsewhere have a spiritual vocation; among the Franciscans for instance. They, the Observantine Friars, were throughout his life his particular friends. To in-cline him to enter either of these orders he had a vivid desire for some sort of training that would prepare him, a spoiled child of fortune, as he con-sidered himself, for the next world. To deter him from entering either of them he had, to begin with, a sense of his own unworthiness, which he expressed in that time-honored formula that it is better to be a pure married man than an impure monk. Then he no doubt was aware, of what we cannot

help being aware in looking back at his career, that
he was most alive in city-life, in city-crowds, most
wise in quick response. It is noteworthy that his
deepest sayings were not thought out in speculation, and aloof, they came spontaneous to More's
lips in the give and take of the occasion. The sparks
of understanding were struck from More by his
contact with the world. And finally, to give him
grave cause for hesitation, he had a well-founded
suspicion that many young men in England were
then taking up a religious life without having received for it a due invitation.

More asked the help of God to lead him to a just
decision as to whether or not he should become a
monk or a priest. Erasmus, who passed through
England, saw how earnestly he prayed. "Meanwhile he applied his whole mind to exercises of
piety, looking to and pondering on the priesthood
in vigils, fasts, and prayers, and similar austerities."

But God had created other men, for him to look
at, and learn from. There were those whom he saw
living, and those who existed still in the picture-
book of history. Among the living was his witty
friend Erasmus, who had become at least more of a
monk than he was fitted to be, for though he had
become merely one of those priests who live somewhat like monks — the Augustinian canons, — he
was near enough a monk to be referred to as such,
and to be able to vent his spleen on monkhood in

general. He for one was thoroughly dissatisfied
with his monkishness. — Yet would not Erasmus
be dissatisfied anywhere? —

Then in freshly written history there was an
extraordinary young layman in Italy who had with
his noble manners, handsome visage, handsome
clothes, noble blood, entered into the world of
philosophers and theologians, more like a meteor
than a man. He had astonished all of Europe by his
brilliance, his rashness, his success. He had carried
the spirit of knighthood, of championship, of
tournament, into the regions, once sober, of the
intellect. He was unprecedented: he was all things
at once. This prodigy, Pico della Mirandola, who
had died when More was very young, was not unlike More in many ways. He knew philosophy and
theology without being a philosopher or a theologian. He was a layman more instructed than
most of the clergy. He had great personal charm.
He was a magician with languages. He was young,
perpetually young. But he was much prouder and
more boastful than More. His faults were such as
might belong to a more aristocratic class than
More's. He had none of More's irony. He had
never been brought up by More's hard-headed
father. He had never humbled himself to become
any one thing, as More had become a lawyer. His
end had been too theatrical for More. He had
thrown himself at the feet of Savonarola, and an-

nounced that he also would make himself a Dominican. Then death had taken him. More studied a
life of Pico written by Pico's nephew. He even
translated it, pored over it, to turn lovingly some
of Pico's sayings into verse. Pico was not his model.

It takes much more humility to ask advice of a
living man, who can speak, than to extract advice
for yourself from the example of another, living or
dead, who is mute, for by that act you declare that
you are not self-sufficient, that you are glad to be
but one of many. We would know, even if we had
no record of it, that More would have availed himself of such a help as a spiritual director. He owned
so thoroughly that medieval wisdom, which taught
that in spiritual guidance a man who consults only
himself consults a blind man, that he would never
have trusted only his own impressions. And we also
have records which prove that he did make use of
such guidance.

These records however do not tell a complete
story. One of the records was discovered quite by
chance. It is the letter of a parish priest, John
Bouge, who tells in digression that he was at one
time (probably from the years 1508 to 1510)
Thomas More's spiritual director. If that letter had
not been unearthed in the 19th century, nobody
would have ever suspected the existence of such a
director. The other indication as to his spiritual
guidance comes from a letter written by More to

the priest and future Dean of St. Paul's Cathedral, John Colet, in the year 1504, in which More writes: "It has been my custom to rely upon your prudent advice, to find my recreation in your pleasant company, to be stirred up by your powerful sermons, to be edified by your life and example, to be guided in fine, by even the slightest indications of your opinions." More goes on to say that Colet is his director, and that Grocyn is his director when Colet is away. This letter, however, may exaggerate the importance of Colet to More, for it is one of those Latin, Ciceronic, letters, such as the humanists liked to write, and which indulged in flattery as a literary exercise.

It cannot be denied, however, that Colet must have been at one time More's director, which is an interesting fact, for it shows how More could derive wise advice from a man much less wise than he. Colet may have been a good spiritual director but he was not a wise man. He was the son of a very rich Lord Mayor of London, who never lost the habit of thinking he could get all things, as the rich can get some things, directly. This made him impatient with human nature, which must be dealt with so indirectly. He also had the scorn which a man of action has for things which do not immediately aid action. Scholastic philosophy was of no use to him. Therefore it was of no use. In regard to giving any man advice as to whether he should

become a monk or not, he was particularly unfitted. He disliked monks in general, and when he
did like them, he liked them for wrong reasons.
His idea of a monastery was a country-house of re-
fined tranquillity, and for such he was constantly
seeking as a refuge into which he might ultimately
retire. Finally he did pay the Carthusians of Richmond the compliment of building a country-house
near them, in which to end his days, but before he
ended his days his days ended. He had to wait until
his arrival in heaven before he could wholly understand monks. When talking to Thomas More he
was still somewhat blind to them.

Colet had, then, his limitations, but it must be
conceded that he was not one of the lax priests, who
were the prevailing fault of the time. He was, on
the contrary, a castigator of them. He was a man of
zeal, vehemence, and courage: a born preacher. He
is usually known for his savage impatience with
simple childlike souls who paid perhaps too much
attention to relics and pilgrimages, but it should
not be forgotten of him that he was also the priest
who set up so lovingly the statue of Christ, the
Child, in his foundation, Saint Paul's School, and
prescribed the prayers to be said before it. He
had his virtues.

And whether we grant his virtues or not, he
must have had some magnetism, or powers of
leadership. He could deflect the whole career of a

man like Erasmus who was a thousand times his superior in intelligence, and could make More write to him such a letter as this: "What can be more distressing to me than to be deprived of your most dear society, after being guided by your wise counsels, cheered by your charming familiarity, assured by your earnest sermons, and helped forward by your example, so that I used to obey your very look or nod."

Furthermore, although unfitted by temperament to perceive some of the individual sensitivenesses of More, he was perfectly able to understand the class to which More belonged, for they were city people, and he was a city man. He knew their thoughts, partook their prejudices, had walked their paths. He had preceded Thomas More at Saint Anthony's School, had preceded him at Oxford. He had caught like More the enthusiasm for ancient letters, for the revival of the study of Greek. Finally as a priest giving advice to a man who had come to him for help, he was fulfilling a function so proper to his state in life, that some of the wisdom of the function no doubt came into his words.

It may very well have been that More at one time in his life made a mistake in over-rating Colet. There is no reason to suppose that he made any mistake in using him as a spiritual director. On the contrary there is every indication that he received

from Colet the advice which God wanted him to
receive. What that advice was we have no direct
way of knowing. We shall never hear its reasonings.
We can judge of what it may have been only by
what happened.

In 1503 King Henry VII sent northward with
much show and pageantry — velvet and red gold
— his daughter to be married to the King of Scotland. But something even more substantial had to
be sent with her, and for her generous dower,
which was to purchase a king for son-in-law,
Henry called upon Parliament to supply a large
gift. In Parliament a young Londoner rose up. He
had been two years before admitted to the Bar,
and had even more recently by the merchants of
London been elected to Parliament. The merchants
had been becoming exasperated by the King's
demands for money. This young man opposed the
excessive grant to the King. His eloquence led
Parliament to pare down the sum, and the King
was so annoyed at having from his own pocket-
book to make up the gift, that he found a way of
fining the young man's father, one hundred pounds.
The young man's name was Thomas More.

Shortly after this a gentleman in Essex, the
father of two daughters began to receive at, and
invite into, his home, this very same young rising
lawyer. The gentleman's name was Colt, and his
elder daughter was called Jane Colt. Thomas More

liked first the looks of the younger sister better than those of the elder, but his heart, noticing the pain that his favoritism caused to the elder daughter, led him to suffer for, then sympathize with, then woo the elder daughter. In 1505 when he was twenty-seven years old he led to his new-bought house in Bucklersbury, London, this elder daughter, Jane Colt, ten years his junior, his bride.

Chapter III

MORE AND ERASMUS

In the year on which More married there came to stay with him a man with whom he was to laugh, as if he were as carefree as a child, for more than ten years, Desiderius Erasmus, so-called of Rotterdam. He was a man quite different from Thomas More in this way: he was all his life a drifter, and More was a man well-rooted. Erasmus had never had even a home in which to be born, nor a city which he could, except by accident, hail as his birth-place. He never could be pinned down to acknowledging with veracity what was his parentage. By best accounts his father was a priest who had no right to be a father at all, and his mother a serving-girl who could not be called wife. Rotterdam was his birth-place solely because it was his mother's place of refuge. And from birth on Erasmus was never to find a place for which he seemed to be made, either geographically or spiritually. He had become a monk because he liked books not because he liked being a monk. Then by various bits of good luck he was enabled to travel, to be a secretary to a bishop, to study

theology in Paris, but he suffered from the hard-
ships of travel, he could be no man's secretary, and
to be a theologian was quite beyond the persever-
ance of his character. So he drifted, and because he
could find no better title to give to himself, called
himself for some years "a poet". He taught others,
he begged, he went to England. He returned to the
continent. And now once again he came to England
and was greeted and housed by the one man of
whom he never complained: Thomas More. He and
Thomas More had one great delight together:
laughter, wit.

Neither of these two laughers was still a school
boy. More was twenty-seven, Erasmus twelve
years older than that, yet it must be acknowledged
that the labor which they undertook together
sounds to us juvenile. It was the translation of the
dialogue of Lucian from Greek into Latin. Not
even the remembrance that Lucian was to them a
third witty man can make us think of such work as
entirely appropriate to these mature minds. We
have forgotten how few people at that time knew
Greek. We have forgotten the great zest that there
was then in speaking well Latin. We have forgotten
that it was almost an article of faith among the
humanists that an exercise in rhetoric was an end
in itself. We need not even be surprised therefore
when Thomas More, besides translating Lucian,
went to the length of writing in Latin additions to

Lucian, when into the mouth of one of Lucian's
characters he put a vehement speech, simply for
the pleasure of writing a speech well, and vehe-
mently, just as if some able and busy lawyer should
now-a-days take the trouble to write a brief for
Mr. Pickwick in Mr. Pickwick's famous law suit.
In this task Erasmus followed him, and competed
with him, and wrote to a priest who was later to be
a monk and then, a martyr, a very pretty letter
about the value of what he and More had done:

"Dearest Richard (Whitford): Although I have
now for many years been immersed in Greek literature, I have recently begun to declaim in Latin, in
order that I might again regain favor with that
tongue, and this at the instigation of Thomas More,
whose eloquence is such (as you know) that he
could win over even an enemy: a man whom I hold
so dear that, if he were to command me to dance
and play ring-around-a-rosy, I should obey him
with pleasure. He is treating this same subject, and
so treats it that there is not an atom therein that
he does not search out and investigate. Unless my
extreme regard for him deceive me, I do not think
that Nature ever fashioned a more able, ready,
aware, or subtle character, or, in a word, one better
endowed with good qualities of all kinds. Add to
this conversational powers commensurate with his
genius, wonderful gaiety of manner, abundance of
wit, but kindly withal, so that you could wish in

him nothing else that pertains to the finished advocate.

"I have not undertaken this task with the idea that I might either equal or surpass such a masterly speaker, but only that I might engage in a battle of minds with this sweetest of all my friends, with whom I am wont so agreeably to mingle the serious with the playful. And I have set myself about this all the more willingly for the reason that I am very desirous that this sort of exercise, than which there is nothing else equally profitable, should at length be restored to our schools. For I see no other reason than this why, in these days of ours, though there are many who turn out to be most eloquent writers, there are so few who do not seem to be actually dumb, whenever the matter in hand demands an orator. Because if, following the advice of Cicero and Fabius, as well as the example of the ancients, we were diligently exercised from childhood in this declamatory practice, there would not be, in my opinion, so great a lack of oratory, so regrettable a state of dumbness, so shameful a condition of halting speech, even in those who make a public profession of oratory.

"I want you to read my Declamation with the thought that it was the result of a few days' trifling, and not a labored composition. I wish you would compare it with More's, so that you may be able to judge whether there is any difference in style between him and myself, two men who are so similar, you are wont to say, in thought, manners, disposition, and love of study, that you deny twin brothers could be found more alike. You certainly love us both equally well, and are equally beloved by us in return. Farewell, my delightful and most jovial Richard. The Country, May 1, 1506."

By the time Erasmus was writing this letter he had left More. The next month he had crossed the channel again, and was experiencing those sufferings in travel from which in his extreme sensibility he was never free. His glands had swollen. His temples throbbed, his ears rang. He was still the drifter.

More, on the other hand, was very happily installed as a Londoner in London. He was so happily married that he could afford to say to someone who asked him why he had married so small a wife, that of two evils one should always choose the lesser. He had taught her, or was teaching her, to read and write Latin, to play the viol, and to sing. Before Erasmus had left England she had presented to More his favorite daughter, Margaret, and during the next four years while Erasmus was in Italy seeking the patronage of the great and at the same time railing against them, she presented him with three more children, two daughters and one son. In 1508 he was for some reason travelling on the continent. We know this because seven years

later he wrote a letter saying how he had visited
Paris and Louvain in that year, and how he had
then investigated carefully the Universities of
those two places, and discovered that even in dialectics they were not superior to Oxford and Cambridge: a fact which shows that, whatever was his
chief mission in Europe, he was still, aside from his
profession, a keen intellectual. It is likely that he
had gone to the continent on some affair of the merchants of London, possibly the foreign merchants,
who were beginning to recognize and ask the aid of
his astuteness, and were beginning to pay him
well.

Then the King died. The loss was not a personal
one to More. On the contrary it was almost a
personal gain for him, for the King had taken
offense at him. It was not even a great sorrow for
London, but it was for London a great pageant.
It was not a death: it was Death.

"First there came riding through the city of
London the sword-bearer of London. . . . Then
the King's trumpeteers, and after them the King's
still minstrel. Then the Florentines, the Venetians,
the Portingalls, the Spaniards, the Frenchmen, the
Esterlings, the gentlemen ushers, the King's
chaplains having no dignity. . . . Then came the
Mayor of London immediately before the chariot,
bearing his mace in his hand. Then came the
chariot wherein the King's corpse lay. Upon which

lay a Picture resembling his Person crowned and
richly apparelled in his Parliament Robe, bearing
in his right hand a sceptre, and in his left hand a
Ball of Gold; over whom there was hanging a rich
cloth of gold pitched upon four staves, which were
set at the four corners of the said chariot, which
chariot was drawn with seven great coursers,
trapped in black velvet, with the arms of England
on every courser, a knight going on foot bearing
a banner in his hand."

Then came the funeral mass at St. Paul's
Cathedral. Then the body was taken to Westminster Abbey.

"The picture was taken from the hearse, and
borne unto Saint Edward's shrine, the King's
chapel, singing this anthem: 'Circumdederunt me
gemitus mortis'. And the said corpse was inclosed,
and all the Royal Ornaments taken from the said
corpse, so that every man might see the said corpse
offered in a coffin of boards, which was covered
with Black Velvet, having a cross of white satin
from the one end of the said coffin to the other;
within the which coffin the very corpse of the King
lay enclosed in lead. Upon the which lead was
written in great letters, chased, Hic iacet Rex
Henricus Septimus."

Scarcely was this funeral over than Erasmus
received a letter from one of his noble patrons in
England, Mountjoy:

"I have no fear but when you heard that our Prince, now Henry VIII whom we call our Octavius, had succeeded to his father's throne, all your melancholy left you at once."

Henry VIII was now King, and such was the hope in this new monarch that Mountjoy could add: "The heavens laugh, the earth exults, all things are full of milk, of honey, of nectar."

Erasmus who was always looking out for a heaven somewhere on this earth, set out for England, for it seemed that heaven had fallen there. He came to stay with More just about the time when More's fourth child, a son, was being born. Out of Erasmus's head while he was More's guest came a different kind of offspring: a book, the one book of Erasmus which is still famous: "The Praise of Folly." Erasmus has a way of explaining in his prefaces that this or that work of his tumbled into being in some idle moment. He explains how the idea of "The Praise of Folly" jiggled into his mind when he was riding mule-back over the Alps on his way back toward England: an account which I am tempted to believe, not because Erasmus's veracity is to be trusted, but because the conception of the book is too much a streak of genius to be arrived at by direct serious effort. The conception is this: it is all very well to talk about reason, but isn't it really folly which keeps the world going? Would we ever have been born at all if our parents hadn't been

just a little bit foolish about one another? Would
we ever have been cared for by a mother if she had
not been blind to our commonplace ugliness? So as
candidates at the universities maintain some thesis
before the world, so let Folly — who is, of course, a
lady because she talks so much — dispute in her
own praise, proving her superiority in what she can
give, and in what she owns: her sovereignty. This
is the conception of a book which came to Erasmus
crossing the Alps. The book itself he put into Latin
words with Thomas More at his side at Bucklersbury, London.

It is hard for some of us to see what glee Thomas
More and Erasmus got by writing for Lucian the
declamations which Lucian himself had not thought
it worth while to write, but we can all envy Erasmus the theme which he had chosen for himself. It
offers such opportunities, such freedoms. After all
it is Folly herself who is speaking, and that clears
the author of any responsibility for what is said.
What would you expect from Folly? Then there is
a double meaning to the word Folly: it can mean
mental derangement; it can mean excess of love.
By wilfully confusing the two meanings, you can
arrive at all sorts of hilarious absurdities. And also
by playing with these two concepts you can catch
sight, in a poet's manner, of deepest truths, and
with the privilege of Shakespeare's fools be occasionally profoundly wise. I haven't the least doubt

that More was delighted to be at the elbow of Erasmus in such a work. Other men like the young King found their recreation in sports like tennis, or in hunting, or in this or that kind of tournament. Even Erasmus was something of a rider. More was bored by most games. Hunting he detested. He rode only when he could not help it. His recreation was an intellectual game like this which Erasmus was playing.

There are some tender sayings in the book: wonderful half-truths: "Folly is what in children makes us love children." "Folly is the cement and principle of friendship." And Folly, when she is talking about men like Marcus Aurelius who somehow because they had no love for any God, for even a false one, are the most unloveable men in history, is really our friend to us as human beings, almost charitable. "To live in folly is to be a man," is not a cruel saying. But for the most part, Folly's tongue is sharp. She dissects us unmercifully: "Since self-satisfaction is a great pleasure and contentment, must we not thank Folly who so often supplies it." Folly shows her hold over kings, priests, lawyers, poets; and her hold over them does not make them loveable but foolish. So goes on the book in its course which might have made it an entire masterpiece, if Erasmus himself had not forgot himself and entered into the book, speaking himself with spleen where

Folly had been speaking hitherto in her own voice.

Erasmus had a grudge against monks, and he had to insist on their defects time and again in order to defend himself for having deserted them. This got him in the habit of pleading his own part anywhere and everywhere, and kept him from ever taking an intellectual and impersonal view of anything. Fasting was bad because it gave him personally indigestion. Fish-eating should be abolished because he had once swooned at the mere smell of fish. So in "The Praise of Folly" he began fighting again his own battles. He was indignant against monks, therefore he made Folly indignant at them, and let her rail at them for what she should have praised them for, their folly. And he certainly was abusive of theologians. He doubts whether it is safe even to speak of them: "You shouldn't agitate a filthy lake nor handle a fetid plant." Having had recently great difficulties in securing a degree in theology (which he never should have tried to receive), and having somewhat surreptitiously at last achieved that honor, he could with real pent-up sincerity give to Folly these words: "They (the theologians) owe me their masterly definitions, their corollaries, their conclusions, their propositions explicit and implicit, with which they are armed to the teeth." As he neared the end of the book, he let Folly

resume her proper banter, let her claim with syllogisms and quotation from scripture that the
saints in glory belong to her. Are they not out of
themselves with joy? Then he closed the book,
entitled it Encomium Moriae, Praise of Folly,
which by a play of words could mean praise of
More, of Morus, his dear fool.

Erasmus then left More, and was employed for
some years at Cambridge University, there pro-
moting the study of Greek, and being there very
well treated by various English prelates, who were
wise enough to perceive his merits, and — what
was more difficult — were patient enough to bear
his fretfulness. The Bishop of Rochester, John
Fisher, later with More to be martyr, was his
particular patron, and the Archbishop of Canterbury went so far as to be the indiscreet benefactor
who presented Erasmus with a living at Aldington,
which was something that Erasmus at first wanted,
and then only wanted in order that he might get
rid of it for money. But in spite of all this kindness,
which was a credit to the churchmen of England,
England was even then not Paradise. Even this
new reign of Henry VIII had not made it that.
And the King's court, as distinguished from the
courts of the bishops, was inclined to be bored
with the beggings of this self-important scholar.
Wrote a friend of Erasmus to him: "I met the
Master of the Rolls and presenting the book of

Plutarch, I showed him what you had written to him about it. He expressed his thanks, briefly, and, as he was busy, or seemed to be, he hurried off himself, and I did not have any other chance of speaking with him." The most Erasmus was ever to receive from the Court of King Henry VIII was to have a battleship named after him, which was one of the best jokes in a hundred years, for Erasmus was not only a pacifist, but the thought of a cannon gave him gripes in his belly. So Erasmus who wanted to be a god, gave up saying that everybody in England knew Greek, that they were the picture of classical polish. He began to say other things, equally eloquent: "For while these people are lascivious bulls and miserly dung-eaters, nevertheless they imagine that they alone feed on ambrosia and Jupiter's brain." Erasmus may have been discovering that England was England, but England was also discovering that Erasmus was always Erasmus.

It is idle to imagine that More had to discover this. He knew it all along. He probably learned it in 1499 when he first met Erasmus, when he had taken Erasmus to see the young prince Henry, and when Erasmus had been piqued because he had not been told beforehand that he would have to make a Latin speech. But Erasmus was not a bore. He was what he was: the least pedantic and most brilliant of all the humanists. More, I believe, really loved him, and could not be bothered about his defects. They were too obvious. He was sorry when he departed.

But there was one thing about that departure: it was more like that of an angel than a man. Not that Erasmus was holy, nor that he was disembodied of a very sensitive body, but he had a singular way of not touching the realities. When he quitted London, he left no vacuum behind him. Life went on as before. Erasmus in London was a companionable phantom. He displaced no air.

But now there came another departure which did leave a vacuum. Jane Colt died, — Uxorcula Mori. More did not wear his heart on his sleeve. We have no ejaculations of his. But twenty years later when he wrote his epitaph, and her epitaph, he used this phrase to describe her, which describes all, Uxorcula Mori — my little wife.

Then an unexpected thing happened. His parish priest, John Bouge, later to become a Carthusian, has written an account of it. "As for Sir Thomas More he was my parishioner at London. I christened him two goodly children. I buried his first wife, and within a month after he came to me on a Sunday night late and there he brought me a dispensation to be married the next Monday without any banns asking. . . . This Mr. More was my ghostly child; in his confession to be so pure, so clean, with great study, deliberation and devotion,

I never heard many such; a gentleman of great
learning, both in law, art and divinity, having no
man like now alive of a layman." More married
again.

No man has ever found fault with this second
marriage as suggesting any weakness in More's
character, for the charm or lack of charm of the
lady — she was a widow with a daughter of her
own, she was older than he, a good housekeeper,
but not beautiful — suggests too unmistakably
that the marriage was one of policy, even if of
misguided policy. But many people have been
shocked and mystified by it, and by its suddenness.
It is just as well that they have been so shocked
and mystified, for it calls attention to a very typical
action of More's. He was not a romantic. He
needed a mother for his four children. He needed
her immediately. He needed someone who had had
experience as a mother. Mistress Alice Middleton,
the lady whom he married, would not only help
him with his four children, but could derive help
from him for her own daughter. The arrangement
would be a fair one. The one virtue requisite in
her, that of being a good manager (when he was so
much away from home), was eminently and even
too much hers. If any of us, further than this, wish
to know why he chose to be married that particular
Monday and to that particular widow, who had the
reputation of being something of a scold, there is

really, in spite of all legends, but one answer. It is none of our affair. More had, as I have said, an extraordinary sense of what was his affair and what was ours. This was his affair, and he never bothered to explain it to us. And we must acknowledge, if we look ahead, that he conducted this affair of his without much bungling.

One thing is certain: More, by this marriage with Mistress Alice Middleton secured an ally who enabled him to pursue his life as he considered it appropriate to pursue it. His life was two-fold, of which one fold may have appeared quite rational to his new wife, and the other somewhat absurd. Yet let it be said of her that she interfered with neither. The part of his life which she could understand, was that part which her previous husband had led, a life in city affairs. In this More was gaining honor and money. He was during the first year of this new marriage invited to read at Lincoln's Inn, which meant that he was illustrious among his fellow-lawyers. And slightly previous to that he had been appointed Under-sheriff of London, which position was a judicial one, not like that of a secondary sheriff, and one which brought him into intimate contact with many of his humbler fellow-citizens, and which won for him from them a great admiration and esteem. But that work occupied him but one day a week: Thursdays. The rest of the time he was a lawyer, a lawyer for and among merchants, and by being that he gained a sum of money, £400 a year, which must be multiplied by perhaps twenty to give it its equivalent worth today. — Surely that pleased the new Mistress More. — But other habits of her husband were less convenient. He had very little sense of worldly dignity. He had a way of going on pilgrimages, sometimes five, six, ten miles, to holy places, shrines of the Virgin, in and about London, and he did not go a-pilgrimaging as Kings did on horseback, nor as some Kings did occasionally in penance, barefoot, but he went plainly, inconspicuously as he was, like one not rich enough for a horse. And his clothes were not elegant, and sometimes he forgot whether he had a hat on or not. And he spent much time in prayer. And he was always at mass early in the morning. And he was serving mass. And sometimes he sang in the choir — and he sang none too well. — And on Fridays he would shut himself up and meditate all day long on the Passion of Our Lord, just as if he couldn't leave that for monks to do. — Monks had nothing to do anyway. — Yet for all this she let him go his way. There was no use trying to change him.

Although More was more detached in spirit from the city life about him than were his neighbors, there was no man more aware than he of what was going on. As I have said, he was most alive when in a crowd, and he knew where the crowds were, and why they were there, and where they were going. He was never in a blurr, he had eyes over all his body. Time and again in his controversial writings when there was a question of fact, he would say: "I was there. I remember that so and so said this." It seemed as if he were an ubiquitous witness of everything that went on in London. And he saw so vividly that his memory did not fail him. The only quality of More that I can recall his having boasted about was his memory.

After he had been married to Mistress Alice for three years, there happened in London an incident to which he was all eyes: the Hunne affair. Richard Hunne was a rich tailor, who, if we may judge by the fact that More's brother-in-law became the administrator of Hunne's property after Hunne's death, may have been a family friend of More's. He was certainly personally known to More. In 1514 this Hunne refused to pay a mortuary fee for the burial of his infant child to the rector of Saint Mary's church, Whitechapel. In fact he took the charge which the rector demanded of him as a pretext for bringing legal suit against that rector for having violated the laws of the land. In so doing he wished to make himself the hero of his fellow-citizens who were then in a quarrel with the local clergy concerning the size of the various fees, and who were, curiously enough, maintaining with in-

dignation that the clergy were disobeying the
instructions of the Pope. These citizens, although
too money-wise, were not irreligious: they were
simply litigious with their privileged neighbors,
and were trying to have a law passed through
Parliament which would reduce some of the ex-
emptions which the clergy had from appearing at
civil courts. The bill was defeated through the in-
fluence of the nobles: a discomfiture which annoyed the townspeople. So they were glad to make
a hero of Hunne.

Now it happened that Hunne was also charged
with heresy. In fact he was under that charge when
he refused to pay for the burial of his infant, and it
was no doubt to try to turn himself from a heretic
into a hero, that led Hunne to bring his law suit
against the rector. The ruse worked. The Londoners were savage against heresy when it took a
visible form like the eating of meat on Fridays,
but when it was a mere affair of doctrine they could
not keep their minds on it. They could keep
their mind on the shillings however. Hunne
personified the grievances of the Londoners.
They were ready to make him the man of the
hour.

Then Hunne failed them. He was not of the stuff
to be their hero. Now exalted, now cast down, he
had moments of audacity, but no fortitude. He
submitted. He paid his fee. He was sent to prison

in a tower of St. Paul's Cathedral: the Lollard's
Tower, still under a charge of heresy.

Then the unfortunate thing happened which
might have been expected of the poor neurasthenic.
He had remorse for his own cowardice. He was
found one morning choked to death, hanging from
a cord. Straightway a popular cry was raised that
there had been foul play, that all this talk about
heresy had been spitefulness of the clergy, and
that Hunne had been murdered. A coroner's jury
declared that Dr. Horsey, the bishop's chancellor,
and two of his officers were guilty of murder. It
took special action by Parliament to rescue Dr.
Horsey and to free him from a charge which rested
neither on likelihood nor evidence.

Now I have not recited this case because there
is any duty on our part to decide whether or not
Hunne was fairly treated. More, from private in-
vestigations, from unexpected encounters with
men who had frequented Hunne's house, was quite
sure that Hunne was a heretic, that is, he was one
who was trying to twist the doctrines of the Universal Church to suit his own temperament. He
was quite sure that Hunne had in despair taken his
own life. But the importance of the incident to us
is that by it More could read the sentiments, the
blindnesses of his fellow-citizens, and the possible
course that their anti-clericalism might take, even
to the abetting of heresy which they detested. He

was reading the book of current events with rare discernment. This was one of those incidents which laid bare the heart of London.

As for his purely intellectual interests, they were by his spiritual and legal activities pretty much crowded out. The only book which he worked on at this time was a book which he never finished — "The History of King Richard III," written — so says the heading at its first printing "by Master Thomas More, then one of the under-sheriffs of London about the year of Our Lord, 1513." It is a book which, curiously enough, seems to have been written both in English and Latin, instead of having been translated from Latin into English as you would expect from the two versions which exist. It can be treated therefore as an exercise, one of the trials of his hand which More made he scarcely knew why. The history may have been an exercise to More, but to us it is a very dramatic bit of writing, filled with discerning sketches of character, and pithy speeches after the manner of the Latin historians. It was a history which showed not only the vigor of Tacitus, but also a native English vividness which made it like an Elizabethan play. No precedent English history, written in the vernacular, could be compared with it, nor was it to have for several generations a successor. More, however, treated it as a failure. He never finished it. He never tried to publish it. He grew discouraged about it, because he was really too busy to go on with it. He had no time to be a Tacitus. Where had he the leisure to be his other-self Erasmus? His predicament he was to describe more eloquently than we can phrase it, in the preface to the "Utopia" which he was soon to write:

"Whiles I do daily bestowe my time about law matters: some to plead, some to hear, some as an arbitrator with mine award to determine, some as an umpire or a judge, with my sentences finally to discuss. Whiles I go one way to see and visit my friend: another way about mine own private affairs. Whiles I spend almost all the day abroad among others, and the residue at home among my own: I leave to myself, I mean to my book no time. For when I am come home I must commune with my wife, chat with my children, and talk with my servants. All the which things I reckon and account among business, forasmuch as they must of necessity be done: and done must they needs be, unless a man will be a stranger in his own house."

But an occasion came to More, and, by chance, the leisure, also, to exercise the Erasmus in him. He was sent to the Low Countries as part of a delegation which was to arrange the rights of the London merchants in Flanders, in relation to those of other merchants. He was in the employ of the King in this embassy, an employ which he had hitherto avoided, liking best to be a private citizen, but he was working for the good of his merchant neighbors, for the good of the city of London, and he had to be in the employ of the King in order to carry on negotiations with the young Duke of Burgundy, then fifteen years old, the man who was later to be the Emperor Charles V. As in all diplomatic conferences each side spends a great deal of time waiting for the other side to make a misstep, so in this conference there was much waiting to be done: a thing which was not pleasant to More, for he did not like to have to spend, as he was forced to, six months away from his family. He missed them. And besides he was being paid while abroad as if he were a churchman or a bachelor, lavishly for his table and lodging, but with no provision for his family left in London. Yet the leisure gave him time to talk, and gave time to the scholars of the continent to talk to him.

The great subject of conversation for him as a humanist was Erasmus's "Praise of Folly." I can scarcely believe that during the preceding centuries many people had not talked with the tone in which Erasmus wrote that book, but until printing came, much that was merely said remained merely said. Printing, which was not yet a half-century old, had printed "The Praise of Folly," made it into a book, a thing which has the air of authority, and suggests that it be taken seriously.

Christendom was not yet used to reading a book as
if it had been written in mere banter, and a Christian listening to "The Praise of Folly" as to something more than after-dinner conversation might
easily become exasperated at it. A serious-minded
scholar, used to the literalness of scholastic argument, and completely unused to watching the expression on a writer's face, and who did not know
Erasmus, was even tempted to grow irate at it.
More had a great deal of practice defending the
book, explaining the fiction of it, and what Folly
was, and what was the relation of Folly to Reason.
But also he had practice in receiving from the parti-
sans of Erasmus — who were often quite as literal
as his enemies, — compliments. He was to them
the Morus given immortality by the "Encomium
Moriae." Never at home had he been so lionized.
And hearing his own wit extolled, his own wit began to stir. He would write something not like
"The Praise of Folly," but suggested by it, and,
in a sense, companion to it.

A few years before this — eight years in fact —
a book had been published in these realms of the
Duke of Burgundy, which had the fascination of a
fairy-tale, — It is not perfectly certain that it was
not a fairy-tale — "The Voyages of Americus Ves-
pucius," — the man who was to give his name to
the new continent, America. "We left the port of
Cadiz," wrote Americus, "four consort ships: and

began our voyage in direct course to the Fortunate
Isles, which are called today the Grand Canaria,
which are situated in the Ocean-sea at the extrem-
ity of the inhabited west." And then he sailed west-
erly and arrived where people lived after a manner
quite different from Europeans. The rhyme-or-
reason of their habits were very hard to discern.
In some of their habits they were logical, in others
absurd, but all the details that Americus chose to
relate of them were both puzzling and picturesque.
"When they go to war, they take their women with
them, not that these may fight, but because they
carry behind them their worldly goods, for a
woman carries on her back for thirty or forty
leagues a load which no man could bear." They
were a naked race which feared the Europeans because they wore clothes. They had no law, they
offered no sacrifice, they were worse than pagans.
Says Americus: "Their manner of living I judge
to be Epicurean." And these people owned their
dwellings in common, and they changed houses at
stated intervals with one another, and they had a
way of getting rid of the sick who had no chance
of recovery, and finally they had one laudable quality quite different from Europeans. Listen to it
described: "The wealth that we enjoy in this our
Europe and elsewhere, such as gold, jewels, pearls,
and other riches, they hold as nothing: and although they have them in their own lands, they

do not labor to obtain them, nor do they value them." Erasmus had written a book describing a land which does exist, Europe, where all things are ruled by Folly. Why not describe a place which does not exist, which could not exist, where people are ruled by Reason? Why not, thought More, write a book to amuse as Americus's book amuses, a book about an island, called No Place: — that is, in Greek, Utopia?

Some people hold that More wrote his "Utopia" with a serious intent at reform, and that he clothed it in fiction in order that he could say things which it would be indiscreet to say openly. That to my mind is putting the whole thing back to front. More started to write the "Utopia" to amuse a small circle of humanists, who liked his Latin, and who were too much above the world to have any interest in its vulgar troubles. But More was not all laughter, and certainly not all unconcern, and he found himself becoming in spite of himself frequently earnest, and at times indignant.

The very story of the making of the book shows this. He began it in Belgium among literary scholars, congenial wits, as a travesty on Americus, as a response to Erasmus, as a prolongation of delightful banter. Then he returned to England. Perhaps his very pondering, perhaps his more serious occupations, perhaps his English companions made him more serious, so he wrote another part to the "Uto-

pia" which he placed first. What is published as the
second part of the "Utopia" was originally written
first, and was much nearer to pure fantasy. We
read the second part both for philosophic play,
and for a delight in the wonders of nowhere. We
read the first part to find out what was wrong with
England in his day. This fact about the two parts
of "Utopia" has always been known by the historians of literature, but at least by the sociologists,
who have appropriated the book, it has been disre-
garded.

As the humanists liked to play lightly and ele-
gantly with serious philosophic notions, so More in
the second part of the "Utopia," plays with the notion of natural man, man with reason alone, unaided by grace, and unillumined by any divine revelation, a notion concerning which the Christian
philosophers of the previous centuries had had
much to say. Now this discussion of More's begins
with an implicit assumption that Erasmus was
right. Folly rules all the men that really exist. You
have to go to NOWHERE to find men who are gov-
erned by reason. Arrived at Nowhere you find a
place which in some of its geographic traits is not
entirely different from England, or from a Londoner's idea of England. It is an island with one great
city, and one important river, up which the tide
comes to the great city, and in the hinterland there
are divisions not unlike English shires, and towns

not unlike English towns. The geographical resemblance to England makes the conduct of the reasonable Utopians all the more striking, and it enables More to write with his tongue in his cheek such perfectly impossible things as this: "Howbeit no man is prohibited or forbid, after the halls be served, to fetch home meate out of the market to his own house. For they know that no man will do it without a cause reasonable." — Just imagine knowing that of any of our brother men. — And then there is this statement about the children. "All the other children of both kinds, as well boys as girls, that be under the age of marriage, do either serve at the tables, or else if they be too young thereto, yet they stand by with marvellous silence." — I should call the silence not marvellous but miraculous. —

If the manners, customs and deeds granted to the Utopians had been entirely according to a philosophic diagram, the book would have lost its carefree quality, and moreover all its verisimilitude. It would have been poor fiction. There are in the accounts of the Utopians details which are almost copied from Americus's Voyage. They make the "Utopia" a parody of a book of travels. Yet of all these things recited, there is nothing absolutely absurd, and I might say that some of them are so reasonable that they are a satire on reason itself, and they prove that man must have something

more than reason to guide him. For instance the
Utopians show the young Utopian girl naked to
the man who wants to marry her before he is allowed to make the choice, which is in one sense
reasonable, and yet to any human intuition gross
and intolerable. And then he has the Utopians very
ungallant in their wars. He has them hire assassins
to kill the leaders of their enemy, which, no matter
how high the assassin may charge, is much cheaper
than paying an army. And then also he has the
Utopians put to death the uncurably sick, when
those sick have given permission for that killing.
These things, I believe More put into his "Utopia"
in the same spirit that Pico della Mirandola offered
to defend theses which he acknowledged to be
false. It was as much as to say: "Let's thrash this
out. Aren't these things reasonable?"

As a matter of fact More had a great deal more
respect for reason than almost any of his humanist
friends. It was an age when reason had been mis-
used, and had fallen into disrespect. And although
some of the habits of the Utopians may be to us
though reasonable yet revolting, for the most part
the Utopians are admirable because they are reasonable, because they have used their reason. For
instance it is because they are reasonable that they
believe in God. They cannot, being reasonable, not
believe in God. Otherwise they would not be human. Thus the Utopians although they are tolerant

of this or that kind of religion, demand that their fellow-citizens at least believe in God, in a future life, in future punishment or reward, otherwise those citizens lose their rights. It would not be reasonable to trust a man who refused to use his intellect. And furthermore this also is true: a man who does not believe in God is, if he is at all reasonable, a wicked man. The "Utopia" has really a great deal to say about reason, for once make man reasonable in his actions, and strange things happen.

Now the Utopians are reasonable people. They are not loveable people. They are not people to be followed. To More they are rather people to be pitied, because they had not received the light of Revelation. But shame on the Christians! They were not using what God had given them, and these Utopians were! The Utopians had been given Reason and they were using it. The Christians had received Faith and Reason, but they were abusing Faith, and not using Reason. So the book, the "Utopia," as was proper, became serious, not in recommending that Christians have a sprinkling of lady priests as they had in Utopia, not in counselling that divorce should be made possible — as was feasible where there was no sacrament of marriage — but in rebuking the Europe of that day for its ten thousand insanities, for its failure in this Commonwealth of Christendom to be reasonable.

Where was the greater folly than in the love of gold so conspicuous in London then, when it was not only amassed as treasure, when it was spread everywhere, by those who had it, for ostentatious ornament, when Cardinal Wolsey decorated his banquet-hall with hundreds of gold platters on the wall, each with a candle in front of it, when to be proud and important, rich men and courtiers garnished themselves with gold cloth and gold chains to show how honorable and honored they were? And where in England was that sanity of the Utopians who, seeing the small utility of gold, used it so appropriately for the marking of thieves and the gilding of chamber-pots?

Sometimes the irony became white hot, like that of Dante about Florence. The Utopians did not make alliances and leagues like other nations. No, they found that among their neighbor nations there was not much constancy in keeping to the leagues that had been formed. In fact the kings in those parts thought themselves above the law of justice, and the princely virtue found nothing unlawful "that it lusted after." So the Utopians thought it best not to make international alliances at all. How very different from Europe! How very different from Christendom. "For" says More (or rather Raphael Hythloday who is telling of Utopia), "For here in Europa, and especially in these parts where the faith and religion of Christ reign-

eth, the majesty of leagues is everywhere esteemed holy and inviolable: partly through the
justice and goodness of princes, and partly at the
reverence and motion of the head Bishops." Such
a remark made at a time when every potentate in
Europe was knifing his neighbor would have turned
any audience for a moment silent.

More had become more earnest in writing of
Nowhere than he had planned, and that earnest-
ness carried him on to write about somewhere. He
described, as I have said, England; made Raphael
Hythloday discuss the crying abuses of that realm.
He wrote that first part of the "Utopia," which —
let me repeat it — though printed first was written
last. What More's personal opinions were, did not
directly appear, for the fiction of a dialogue was
sustained, which ended not with a conclusion, but,
after the manner of the humanists, with a dinner.
Yet there is no disguising that the woes of England
to More's eyes were first the vagabondage caused
by the disbanding of armies, and by the dismissing
arbitrarily of vast groups of servitors by the mag-
nates; second, the severe penalties of the law which
punished the thief of a handkerchief the same as
the murderer of a man: both with death; and third,
the dispossession of the small landowners of their
lands by the great landlords, all for the sake of
sheep grazing. "Forsooth your sheep" — so says
Hythloday to Cardinal Morton, "that were wont

to be so meek and tame, and so small eaters, now, as I hear say, be become so great devourers and so wild, that they do eat up, and swallow down the very men themselves. They consume, destroy, and devour whole fields, houses, and cities. For look in what parts of the realm doth grow the finest, and therefore dearest wool, there noblemen, and gentlemen, yea and certain abbots, holy men, God wot, — not contenting themselves with the yearly revenues and profits that were wont to grow their forefathers and predecessors of their lands, nor being content that they live in rest and pleasure, nothing profiting, yea, much annoying the weal public, leave no ground for tillage: they enclose all in pastures; they throw down houses; they pluck down towns; and leave nothing standing but only the church, to make it a sheep-house."

More had begun by trying to write the same kind of a book as Erasmus's "Praise of Folly," but the book which he wrote has only as much relation to the "Praise of Folly," as More's character has to that of Erasmus. And how different have been the fates of the two books! "Utopia" has given a word to all our European languages: the word Utopia. It has been translated and translated from its original Latin, and has been read and misread and re-read like the great masterpieces: Dante's "Divine Comedy" and Shakespeare's plays. The only one of the humanists who chose to be not a claimant for their much-sought-after immortality is the only one who wrote a book which is still indubitably alive.

Chapter IV

MORE'S HOUSEHOLD

More had introduced his own self as one of the speakers in the Utopia. His most animated conversation had taken place in that part of the book which concerned England, and his subject had not been so much the nature of England's miseries, as the utility of philosophers in general. According to Plato, kings should be philosophers. According to Erasmus, kings, if they were philosophers would be very poor kings. According to Hythloday — whose name had been twisted from the Greek to mean babbler, — philosophers were useful to make good conversation: babble. "This school philosophy" he said "is not unpleasant among friends in familiar communication, but in the counsels of kings, where great matters be debated and reasoned with great authority, these things have no place." More disagreed with Plato, with Erasmus, with Hythloday; he had what you might call a very practical, London, English, solution of the difficulty.

He began by acknowledging that the school philosophy which thinks all things suitable for all places has indeed no place near to kings, and practical rulers. "But there is" he adds "another philosophy more civil, which knoweth, as you would say, her own stage, and thereafter ordering, and behaving herself in the play that she hath in hand, playeth her part accordingly with comeliness, uttering nothing out of due order and fashion. And this is the philosophy that you must use. Or else while a comedy of Plautus is playing, and the vile bondmen scoffing and trifling among themselves, if you should suddenly come upon the stage in a Philosopher's apparell and rehearse out of 'Octavia' the place wherein Seneca disputeth with Nero: had it not been better for you to have played the dumb person, than by rehearsing that, which serveth neither for the time nor place, to have made such a tragical comedy or gallimaufry? For by bringing in other stuff that nothing appertaineth to the present matter, you must needs mar and pervert the play that is in hand, though the stuff that you bring be much better. What part soever you have taken upon you, play that as well as you can, and make the best of it. And do not therefore disturb and bring out of order the whole matter, because that another, which is merrier and better cometh to your remembrance. So the case standeth in the commonwealth, and so it is in the consultations of kings and princes. If evil opinions and naughty persuasions can not be utterly and quite plucked out of their hearts, if you can not even as you would remedy vices, which use and custom hath confirmed: yet for this cause you must not leave and forsake the commonwealth: you must not forsake the ship in a tempest, because you can not rule and keep down the winds. No, nor you must not labor to drive into their heads new and strange informations, which you know well shall be nothing regarded with them that be of clean contrary minds. But you must with a crafty wile and a subtle train study and endeavor yourself, as much as in you lieth, to handle the matter wittily and handsomely for the purpose, and that which you can not turn to good, so to order it that it be not very bad. For it is not possible for all things to be well, unless all men are good. Which I think will not be yet this good many years."

All things were not well. More, although he was personally prosperous, knew they were not all well. Erasmus was different. To him things were all right or all wrong, according as they were all right or all wrong with him. One day he could write: "Where is gladness or repose? Wherever I turn my eyes I only see disaster and harshness. And in such a bustle and clamor about me you wish me to find leisure for the work of the Muses." But the next day when flattery and good digestion in alliance had soothed him, he could cry out: "Peace, happiness impends. Learning will right all." More had not these ups and downs. There was no peace in Christendom. There was not even any prospect of peace while the kings were intriguing as they were. There was no peace between Christendom and the Turks. There could not be, unless the Christian princes should become willing to lay aside their quarrels for the good of Christendom as a whole. Happiness? Well, in England it was not happiness that the poor were becoming poorer, the rich richer, and that the economic changes were driving out the small farmers, enclosing the common lands, and turning the tilled land to pasturage, causing the sheep, as he put it, to devour men. Learning? Was it really so flourishing? Had not this study of Greek, of which he thought so much, encountered opposition after opposition at the Universities? At Oxford there were street-fights between those students who favored Greek and those who did not, wars between the Greeks and the Trojans as they called themselves. It was indeed a sick world, sicker even than usual.

So easy is it for a man who enjoys private prosperity to forget the common woes, that it is well to remark with leisure and meditation, just how much disturbed More was about the troubles of others, and how clear-sighted he was into abuses which did not concern him directly. Otherwise we might think that his humility in doing no more

than his part was due to indifference, or blindness.
More never had his house sacked in the wars, nor
was there any probability that England would
suffer invasion. His thought of peace had nothing
to do with his own personal safety or personal
fortune. Yet his preoccupation for the peace of
Europe was profound. His interest in the yeomen
of England, the small farmers, was also equally
unselfish. He was not even a country-man. He had
to look through London houses to see the country,
and over the heads of his fellow-citizens to see
his brother-men who lived there. He was hedged in
by city prejudices, deafened by city talk, drawn
by personal friendship with merchants to sympathize with wool-merchants, rather than growers
of corn, yet if there is any class in England of whose
troubles he thought most, it was of the farming
class. This was the dispassionate shrewdness of
More which looked irrespective of private affection
to the public problem. His eyes which according to
Erasmus were grayish blue with spots in them that
betokened talent, had the power of being, though
tender, yet wonderfully penetrant.

As for doing something to reform the evils in
England, he would begin where nobody wants to
begin, where it is obviously useless to begin, where
it was his part to begin: at the beginning. More
was not omnipotent. He did not hold the green
fields of England in his hand, but he had a certain

sovereignty over himself. He would begin with himself.

In reforming himself there were some vices which he did not have much to attend to: gluttony for instance. He was naturally in his diet temperate. "I never saw anyone so indifferent about food," says Erasmus. "Until he was a young man he delighted in drinking water, but that came to him by way of his fathers. Yet not to seem singular or morose, he would hide his temperance from his guests by drinking out of a pewter vessel beer almost as light as water, or often pure water. It is the custom in England to pledge each other in drinking wine. In doing so he will merely touch it with his lips, not to seem to dislike it, or to fall in with the custom. He likes to eat corned beef and coarse bread much leavened, rather than what most people count delicacies. Otherwise he has no aversion to what gives harmless pleasure to the body. He prefers milk diet and fruits, and is especially fond of eggs." Let us not give Thomas More credit for drinking water, but we can give him credit for diluting it with beer. To drain such a draught must have been a real penance.

More went beyond the temperance of the philosophers in the treatment of his body. He practised austerities and mortifications to which no man would ask his body to submit, unless he understood the open secrets which a Christian understands, unless he looked forward to heaven and feared hell, and saw the Crucifix as the centre of the world and of history. More wore a hair-shirt, and he scourged himself with whips and knotted cords.

But mostly he put himself in order not through bodily punishment, but through meditations of his mind and heart, through prayers, through the frequenting of the Sacraments. He attended daily Mass, he also recited daily the Seven Penitential Psalms, the Litany of the Saints, and various other psalms, "particularly that beginning Beati Immaculati". He made up various prayers for himself both in Latin and English. After a day on which some great event had happened, he always meditated long at night on that event that seemed so great, and when he foresaw some great event ahead, or when some day of terrible decision dawned, he would on that important day, for his enlightenment, for his strength, and in order to be at one with God and all his fellow-faithful, receive Holy Communion.

Also, although he was not in charge of the universe, nor even of a kingdom, he was in charge of a family. So he played the governor of his own Englishman's castle, and tried within it to create that earthly paradise of which his brother humanists so much dreamed. Poor literary men, they longed above all for a place where they could write undisturbed, and where they could endlessly and

gracefully talk! Seldom in life did they come near
to such a place, but in their writings they frequented it. Their dialogues, which were their
favorite form of literature, were always imagined
as taking place in some delicious quietude, a garden preferably, where it did not rain, where the
table was set, where there struck no clock. Sometimes such a garden was actually possessed for a
moment or two by a humanist, or for the sake of a
delightful letter to a friend, and for the literary
exercise of describing it, a humanist would imagine
he had secured it. The Italian humanist Bembo,
later to be Cardinal Bembo, described his garden
as if it were really come true. "I do not think of
law suits," he says, "I read and write when I
please; I ride and walk; and not seldom I take an
airing in a small wood at the end of my garden.
From this spot, in every way most delicious and
lovely, I often gather with my own hands a salad
for the first course of my supper, or a large basket
of strawberries which perfume my mouth, and
indeed the whole table. . . . Then I have only to
go a fair stretch in my little boat, at first down a
meandering streamlet, which ripples past the
house, and then along the Brenta, into which,
after a short course, my streamlet flows — a
pleasant and noble river; and this in the evening
time when running water rather than land delights
me." We are all enchanted by such an account,

but the care-taker in us can not help asking how such a place could have existed. Who was the housekeeper? Who behind the scenes saw that the horse was shod, and the trees pruned, and the boat on the Brenta baled out? Here was monastic calm without monastic discipline. Can it so be bought? Truly this place was nowhere. But Thomas More, living in London, and not leaving behind his citizen shrewdness, tried to create such a paradise, not out of nothing, but out of what he had: his family household.

It was towards the gaining of such an impossible paradise that More had taught his first wife to play the viol and write Latin. He now taught his second wife, already growing old, to learn to play the harp, the lute, the monochord and the flute. If he could accomplish this with his second wife, what could he not accomplish with his children? None of his children died, which was for that day a rare fortune. All of them he educated with a personal and loving care, but also through wisely-chosen tutors. He would make them intellectual. Three of them were girls, and the fourth, the last, — the boy, — was the least intelligent, so it was with girls that he began and mostly worked. Yet girls or no girls, he would have his children know Latin, Greek, astronomy. "In that house," says Erasmus "you will find no one idle, no one busied in feminine trifles. Titus Livius is ever in their hands.

They have advanced so far that they can read such authors and understand them without a translation, unless there occurs some such word as would perplex myself." More felt called upon to defend this putting of heavy volumes of Livy into the hands of pretty daughters. Wrote he to a young ecclesiastic, Gunnell, who acted as tutor to his children: "Since erudition in women is a new thing and a reproach to the sloth of men, many will gladly assail it, and impute to literature what is really the fault of nature, thinking from the vices of the learned to get their own ignorance esteemed as virtue. On the other hand, if a woman (and this I desire and hope with you as their teacher for all my daughters) to eminent virtue should add an outwork of even moderate skill in literature, I think she will have more real profit than if she had obtained the riches of Croesus and the beauty of Helen." And then because More hated to appear as putting himself as first in anything, he showed that he was not an innovator. Look at the "excellent matrons" and "noble virgins" whom Saint Jerome took such care to make learned.

But the question before More was deeper than the special one of the education of girls, it was the question of the relation of all learning to vainglory. He had seen no end of what to him was very hateful — intellectual pride; and he could not through friendship be blind to the pedantry of all

but a few of the humanists. What good would it
really do to his children to have them know Latin
and Greek except to puff them up? More's answer
was that the study of books rightfully turns our
attention toward things spiritual, and thus weans
us from dependence on public praise, and that this
study would make us humble, therefore, if only
our teachers conducted us wisely. He continued to
the tutor: "But, dear Gunnell, the more I see the
difficulty of getting rid of this pest of pride, the
more do I see the necessity of setting to work at it
from childhood. For I find no other reason why
this evil clings so to our hearts, than because
almost as soon as we are born, it is sown in the
tender minds of children by their nurses, it is cul-
tivated by their teachers, and brought to its full
growth by their parents; no one teaching even
what is good without, at the same time, awakening
the expectation of praise, as if the proper reward of
virtue. Thus we grow accustomed to make so much
of praise, that while we study how to please the
greater number (who will always be the worst), we
grow ashamed of being good (with the few). That
this plague of vainglory may be banished far from
my children, I desire that you, my dear Gunnell,
and their mother and all their friends, would sing
this song to them, and repeat it, and beat it into
their heads, that vainglory is a thing despicable,
and to be spit upon; and that there is nothing more

sublime than that humble modesty so often praised
by Christ; and this your prudent charity will so
enforce as to teach virtue rather than reprove vice,
and make them love good advice instead of hating
it. To this purpose nothing will more conduce than
to read them the lessons of the ancient Fathers,
who, they know, cannot be angry with them, and,
as they honor them for their sanctity, they must
needs be much moved by their authority. If you
will teach something of this sort, in its proper relation to their lesson in Sallust — to Margaret and
Elizabeth, as being more advanced than John and
Cecily — you will bind me and them still more to
you. And thus you will bring about that my children, who are dear to me by nature, and still more
dear by learning and virtue, will become most dear
by that advance in knowledge and good conduct."

But Gunnell of Cambridge University could
never have made More's learned children humble.
That required the master of the house rather than
the master of studies. More saw to it that God was
the centre of their life, not any mere idol of human
perfection. Stapleton, the priest, who was born the
day More died, and who knew so well More's
children, has told to us the devotions of that house.
"Whenever he was at home, it was his custom to
gather together every evening before bed-time a
large part of his household for night prayers. Together all would kneel and recite the three psalms:

'Have mercy on me, O God', 'To Thee, O Lord, have I lifted up my soul', and 'May God have mercy on us', the 'Hail, holy Queen' with its prayer; and finally the 'Out of the depths' for the dead. He continued this practice even when he was Lord Chancellor." — All of this sounds merely like the common custom of any age less egotistic than ours, when families prayed as families and not only as individuals, but what Stapleton tells next is more extraordinary. — "At table a passage of sacred Scripture was read with the commentaries of Nicholas of Lyra or some other ancient writer. One of his daughters would be the reader. The passage from Scripture was intoned in the ecclesiastical or monastic fashion, and was ended with the words 'and do thou, O Lord, have mercy on us', as in religious houses. The reading was continued until a sign was given, and then More would ask one of the company how this or that passage should be understood."

But More knew his family were not monks, and he did not want them to imagine any such thing, so "afterwards More in his inimitable way would suggest some lighter topic, and all would be highly amused. Pattenson, More's fool, would then join in the conversation."

More's lighter vein certainly kept the household what it was, and was to the household necessary. False solemnity, false sanctity, and all other forms of falsity, would have followed without it; and all the resulting self-importance would have brought quarrel after quarrel: jealousy, no joy. For More's lighter vein reduced all things to their proper size: even his wife's complaints which he ever answered with banter. Erasmus has told us with admiration of how More ruled his house by his nimble spirit, by his laughter; but would that Erasmus, or anybody else, could restore to us the sound of his voice, the tone of his voice when he said these things; the delicacy and slyness of his jests! Erasmus never tried to record his sayings. Such things can never be repeated. Is it fair then to print here as a sample of his humor, a jest written originally in rhetorical Latin to his daughter that it be read by her as part of her literary exercise? Yet here is such a passage. "Your zeal for knowledge binds me to you almost more closely than the ties of blood. I rejoice that Mr. Drew has returned safe, for I was anxious, as you know, about him. If I did not love you so much, I should be really envious of your happiness in having so many and such excellent tutors. But I think you have no longer any need of Mr. Nicholas, since you have learnt whatever he had to teach you about astronomy. I hear you are so advanced in that science that you can not only point out the pole-star or the dog-star, or any of the constellations, but are able also — which requires a skilful and profound astrologer — among all those leading heavenly bodies, to distinguish the sun from the moon."

More also humbled his household by making it neighbor to all mankind by hospitality. Although his daughters were so extraordinarily intellectual that they were asked to carry on a philosophic disputation before the King of England, yet their house was not really a glass-case which kept them apart and under observation as an eighth wonder of the world. Their first house was in Bucklersbury, St. Stephen's Parish, Walbrook, London, and was undoubtedly their smallest house. Their next house they bought from an Italian merchant, Bonvisi, who of all the merchants of London was the most intimate with More. It was in Crosby Place. Their last house was the greatest. It was in Chelsea, which then but looked at London. It was in the country, and dominated a plot of land on which stood farm buildings, and which was large enough to give More space to have a private chapel, and for his delightful freedom of spirit, a menagerie. Says Erasmus: "He is fond of animals of all kinds, and likes to watch their habits. All the birds in Chelsea come to him to be fed. He has a menagerie of tame beasts, a monkey, a fox, a ferret, and a weasel. He buys any singular thing which is brought to him. His house is a magazine of curiosities, which he delights in showing off." This last house of More most conformed to his ideal. It was the house which he had commanded to be built. But all the houses had a spaciousness of spirit about them. They greeted all men: poor, rich, wise, foolish, kin, and stranger, as not outsiders.

Picture the visits of the intellectuals to More. They were frequently drawn to Chelsea, says Ellis Heywood, both by its proximity to the city, and "by the admirable character of its owner." Their discourses there were "attended with great profit to each other." And the same Heywood who knew such gatherings recounted how the scholars "retired after dinner into a garden, distant about two stone-throws from the house, and went all together to stand upon a small green eminence, and gaze on the prospect. The place was wonderfully charming; both from the advantages of its site, for from one part almost the whole of the noble city of London was visible; and from another, the beautiful Thames, with green meadows, and woody eminences all around; and also for its own beauty, for as it was crowned with an almost perpetual verdure, it had flowering shrubs, and the branches of fruit trees which grew near, interwoven by nature herself, and much more noble than any other work, inasmuch as it gave entire satisfaction, whereas the copies of beautiful objects leave the mind rather in desire than in content."

Also the King of England would come to More's

house, and would arrive unexpected to dinner, and would walk in More's garden with More, his arm thrown over More's shoulder. And the Duke of Norfolk — when More was Lord Chancellor — would come to his house, and Thomas Cromwell, the schemer, would drop in to size More up. And the poor came begging. And poor neighbors would eat often at his table, and though he gave few banquets to the rich and noble, yet the poor neighbors would often sit at his table, and others of the infirm, poor, and old were lodged at a special house of his in Chelsea. And not only to meals did he invite the unfortunate, but even with an apparent incongruity he made them of his household for indefinite periods. He adopted a poor widow named Paula who had spent all her money in a way which perhaps touched his conscience and sympathy, — litigation. He adopted also in a more real sense a distant relative, Margaret Giggs, a young girl, who eventually married the Greek scholar, and future physician, John Clements. And John Clements, himself, was often one of the members of the household, and so was Harris, the secretary, who had a hard time keeping More dressed in decently new clothes, — especially shoes — and various tutors were there, and servants, men and women, all of whom More treated like his own children. And in his house was a chaplain, later a martyr. And, of course, in his house was Mistress More,

and Mistress More's daughter by her first marriage, and then the husband of that step-child, and
More's own daughters, Margaret, Elizabeth, and
Cecily, and eventually their husbands, and his own
son John, and John's wife, Anne Cresacre, and during certain periods More's own father, and More's
father's second and third wives, and, — I should
not forget him — More's fool, Henry Pattensen,
who had a license to speak folly with all freedom.
Such a household was too much like the universe
to be precious.

The real proof of how well More conceived of and
conducted his household lies not in the praise which
he won from so many of his astounded contem-
poraries, but in what it produced: Margaret Roper,
his daughter, or rather the affection between More
and that daughter. Margaret Roper was a wonderful scholar. She was philologist enough to
correct the Greek text of Saint Cyprian, and to
suggest readings of it which even men could not
think of, but which were so ingeniously conjec-
tured that they were accepted as true. She was
like her father in intellectual talents. She was like
him also in charm. "She was to her servants" says
Cardinal Pole who knew her "meek and gentle, to
her brothers and sisters most loving and amiable,
to her friends steadfast and comfortable, and
would give very sound counsel, which is a rare
thing in woman." She married William Roper, who

was to be her father's first biographer, and was to him a "debonair and gentle" wife. To her father she was all affection, all understanding.

She understood his jests, she understood his pieties. She alone was entrusted to know that he wore a hair-shirt. She alone was given the secret work of washing it. She could be trusted not to laugh at such things. As for the other daughters, — excellent daughters — they could not help bursting into laughter when on a hot summer's day the disarranged clothing of their father disclosed the unusual shirt. She in his imprisonment was to be most constant, most loving to him. She was to kiss him, the last of his daughters, and the last of persons on earth she was to receive his kiss except the executioner. And when he was dead, and his parboiled head was stuck on a pike on London Bridge, it was she who bribed the man who should have thrown it into the water to give it to her instead. It was she who treasured that head.

More wrote many letters to Margaret Roper, some about her studies when she was young, and others about his decisions when he was in the Tower, when she was older, but when their love for one another was the same. There is a very beautiful letter written from More to her, during the period in between. She was about to be confined. "In your letter you speak of your approaching confinement. We pray most earnestly that all may

go happily and successfully with you. May God
and our Blessed Mother grant you happily and
safely a little one like to his mother in everything
but sex. Yet let it by all means be a girl, if only she
will make up for the inferiority of her sex by her
zeal to imitate her mother's virtue and learning.
Such a girl I should prefer to three boys. Good-bye,
my dearest child."

At one time More almost lost his daughter. It
was the "sweating sickness" that took her. The
physicians despaired of her life. Her father was
heavy with anguish, and went up into the new
chapel which he had built, and prayed to God's
omnipotence for his daughter's recovery. While at
prayer More bethought him of certain medical
treatment which as a layman, and as a very dis-
creet layman, it was scarcely for him to suggest.
But he did suggest it to the doctors, and the
doctors approved, and when applied to his daughter it had an astounding effect. To the surprise of
the doctors the girl recovered. Margaret Roper was
the pearl in More's life. She deserved to be the
pearl. She was his first child, the child of his heart,
the dearest of daughters, the most secret of friends.

What a household then it was that More had
created! It was so happy that it might have made
him forget heaven. Yet although he enjoyed its
graciousness to the fullest, and was always longing
for it when away from it, he detached himself from

it in spirit by his meditations. With that very most-beloved daughter of his he wrote a treatise on The Four Last Things: Death, Judgment, Heaven and Hell. He wrote it, I say, with her, but really separate from her, although simultaneously. They both tried their hand at the same subject. Margaret's attempt is lost. Her father's was not finished. It was a gay yet mordant work of self-mockery, deriding himself and others for thinking they held in their hands anything permanently in this world. He delighted in his household. He delighted in the ownership of his house. Perhaps that is why he wrote so many scathing pages about covetousness. "And no marvel though covetousness be hard to heal. For it is not easy to find a good time to give them counsel. As for the glutton, he is ready to hear of temperance, yea and preach also of fasting himself, when his belly is filled, — the lecherous, after his foul pleasure past, may suffer to hear of continence, and abhorreth almost the other by himself. But the covetous man, because he never ceaseth to dote upon his goods, and is ever alike greedy thereupon, whoso giveth him advice to be liberal seemeth to preach to a glutton for fasting when his belly is empty and gapeth for good meat, or to a lusty lecher when his leman is lately light in his lap. Scantly can death cure them when he cometh. I remember me of a thief once cast at Newgate, that cut a purse at the bar when he should be hanged on the morrow; and when he was asked why he did so, knowing that he should die so shortly, the desperate wretch said that it did his heart good to be lord of that purse one night yet."

With what spirit unmiserly More taught himself to hold to his possessions, we can tell by his letter to his wife when during the full tide of his prosperity his barns owing to the carelessness of a neighbor were burned down:

"Mistress Alice: — In my most heartiest wise I recommend me to you.

"And whereas I am informed by my son Heron, [that is his son-in-law who had married Cecily] of the loss of our barns and our neighbors' also with all the corn that was therein, albeit, saving God's pleasure, it is great pity of so much good corn lost, yet sith it hath liked him to send us such a chance, we must, and are bounden, not only to be content, but also to be glad of his visitation. He sent us all that we have lost; and sith he hath by such a chance taken it away again, his pleasure be fulfilled. Let us never grudge thereat, but take it in good worth, and heartily thank him as well for adversity as for prosperity. And peradventure we have more cause to thank him for our loss than for our winning. For his wisdom better seeth what is good for us than we do ourselves.

"Therefore I pray you be of good cheer, and take

all the household with you to church, and there
thank God both for that he hath given us and for
that he hath taken from us, and for that he hath
left us, which if it please him he can increase when
he will. And if it please him to leave us yet less, at
his pleasure be it. I pray you to make some good
ensearch what my poor neighbors have lost, and
bid them take no thought therefor; for and I
should not leave myself a spoon, there shall no
poor neighbor of mine bear no loss by any chance
happened in my house.

"I pray you with my children and your household be merry in God, and devise somewhat with
your friends what way were best to take for provision to be made for corn for our household, and
for seed this year coming; and if ye think it good
that we keep the ground still in our hands. And
whether ye think it good that we do so or not, yet
I think it were not best suddenly to leave it all up,
and to put away our folk off our farm till we have
somewhat advised us thereon. Howbeit, if ye have
more now than ye shall need, and which can get
them other masters, ye may then discharge us of
them. But I would not that any man were suddenly
sent away he wot not whither.

"At my coming hither, I perceived none other
but that I should tarry still with the King's Grace.
But now I shall, I think, because of this chance
yet leave this week to come home and see you:

and then shall we further devise together upon all things what order shall be best to take. And thereas hearty fare you well, with all your children, as ye can wish.

"At Woodstock the third day of September 1528 by the hand of your loving husband,

Thomas More."

Chapter V

There were in England in the time of More two governments which fronted each other with similar majesty as two palaces might front each other on a public square. One of them was the ecclesiastical government, the other the civil; or — to use the names which in old time they went by — one was the Spiritualty, the other the Temporalty. The former guarded man's eternal interests, the latter his temporary. The former was the more important, first for the general reason that in the Middle Ages, as in almost all the periods of history, man's final destiny was considered as more important than his earthly one, but also for at least two other reasons: the Church was universal, the civil government was local; the Church had established the state, rather than the state the Church.

This dualism of government does not survive in a complete sense in any country of our modern world. It succumbed in that revolution which set the temporal higher than the spiritual. The civil government with its great physical force, and its moral force of patriotism, claims the sole authority, and the theological quarrels of half a thousand years have cast masses of the population in doubt as to which is really the bishop's palace, and as to whether there should be any such thing at all. But though the ancient dualism of government may not have survived, the effects of it do survive. Had the Middle Ages lacked its dual system of government there would have sprung up in Western Europe the divinized monarchies of the East, where the king is king-priest, and all our occidental liberties, which we have so abused, would never have been our inheritance.

These two forms of government not only did their governing; they also provided stairways of ambition to men of ability. In the healthiest days of the Middle Ages men of talent had generally gravitated toward the Church. Not only was the ecclesiastical government more stable and more towering than the civil government, and more honorable, but access to its places of authority was more possible to the man who happened not to be nobly born. Just lately however, the royal service had become more tempting. Kings had become more powerful. With gun-powder and money they could rise high above the heads of their vassals, they could even lord it over the Church. The kings of Europe, moreover, were looking for men of talent not only to embellish their courts, but to make firm by wile and guile their authority.

More was tempted neither by the high places in the Church nor by those in the civil state. Indeed from the former he was cut-off: he was a layman. The authority, and greatness, and power, which the latter had to offer him, rather repelled than attracted him. He feared the pride of high place. He liked the simplicity, and the freedom, and the leisure of private life. If he had ambition in a worldly sense, it was that of a man of letters, for fame, but such an ambition he had never coddled. He had mocked it. The only high place which he would have accepted as a matter of course would have been a judgeship, for that belonged to his career as a lawyer. It was a professional satisfaction. He was glad to be, what he was for the moment, Under-sheriff of the city of London.

He had, in fact, shown openly his wish to stay where he was. In the year 1515, he had gone to the continent to arrange the trade-privileges of the London merchants, an errand which brought him for a moment into the King's employ. During that mission he had not only written his Utopia, but had so well conducted negotiations that the eye of the King's new minister, Lord Chancellor Wolsey, Archbishop of York, newly created Cardinal, fell upon him. Wolsey was bent on running England with a new efficiency, and needed More's talents. So the King offered More £100 a year as pension, to keep him in the Court's pay. More declined the offer. It was impossible for him, he said, to remain Under-sheriff of London, to be trusted by his clients in the city, if he were also in the King's pay. He would have to choose between going to the Court or staying with the City. Unless forced to it, he preferred staying with the City.

But soon he was to be forced to it, for he made himself more and more conspicuous. In 1516 he argued a case before Cardinal Wolsey in the Court of the Star Chamber which gave Wolsey an even higher opinion of him. The legal quarrel was this: a ship belonging to Pope Leo X had been blown into the port of Southampton, and had been claimed by Henry VIII as forfeit to him. The Pope's ambassador had chosen More, not for his piety, but for his legal acumen, as the foremost lawyer in London to argue the Pope's cause. More explained the English law with wonderful dexterity to the foreigner. He defined the points at issue so well, and pleaded so ably his side of the controversy, that the Pope won the ship, and More won the fame of the day. Wolsey was more bent than ever on having More at Court.

The next year, — in its Spring at least, — More was still in London. There came to pass then that Evil May Day in which More took such an active part. Riots broke out in London against the foreign artisans: the Flemings, the French. Two London apprentices, fore-runners of the best English novelists, had invented a tale, according to which a French tailor had stolen from an English husband an English wife. Not only had he lured her to come and live in his house, but he had persuaded her to come not only with her person, but with her husband's belongings, her English husband's good English plate. When the outraged Englishman had protested before the law, the Frenchman had brought counter-suit charging that the Englishman owed him for the board of his wife. This story, which for fiction deserves a prize, did, when it was taken for truth, start a riot. A mob of apprentices, credulous women, excitable men, began to pour through the streets, angry first for the particular outrage of the story, but also proclaiming in general that it was not just that foreigners should be earning good English money. Under this apparent respectability, there was of course the cruelty of a mob blind for destruction, seeking murder as a huntsman seeks his quarry. Frenchmen, Flemings were killed. Houses were sacked, burned, and the City which was proud of its order and of its own liberties with which even the King could not interfere, was in disgrace for not being able to show itself worthy of its name. In this difficult moment the merchants, the aldermen, the Lord Mayor, looked to Thomas More. He was the man whom they knew the mob would be most likely to listen to. They called on their Under-sheriff.

More responded to the call. He, who seldom mounted a horse, and who preferred not to be in the foreground, on this occasion broke his rule. He rode out to meet the apprentices, as a man who was known to be a just man and could expect deference. He talked to them. They listened. They seemed about to cease to be a mob. As a matter of fact, they did somewhat cease their violence, even though they continued refractory. But even though More did have but half a triumph with them, he at least won the fame, which lasted popularly well down into the days of Elizabeth, of being the hero of Evil May Day: not only the man who quieted the mob, and brought it to reason, but also the man who saved many an apprentice from execution, for the King by an ancient law which was rediscovered for the purpose threatened the lives of many of these rioters. Some of them, no doubt, deserved stiff punishment. Certainly some of them got it. Eleven gallows were set up in the street, and twenty-one persons — according to Arnold, the London haberdasher, who kept a journal — were "hanged, drawn and quartered," one of them "Lincoln, a broker." And worse impended, as Arnold also describes. "And then came in the King, with his Lords Spiritual and Temporal, and the King sitting in his seat royal, all the prisoners came before him, and kneeled down, and cried with a loud voice, mercy and grace, two or three times, and then the Mayor, Aldermen, and citizens, kneeled for the same petition, and the Lords Spiritual and Temporal kneeled before the King for pardon, upon all which petitions the King then granted pardon, and those that was judged to death had their charters." Now of those citizens kneeling next the aldermen was Thomas More. He was that strange humanist who could keep his head in a turmoil, and think when people were shouting. To most of the humanists, the populace were extremely repugnant. They scarcely had souls, they were unlettered, and letters were salvation. To Erasmus, they were, above all, ill-smelling. Thomas More was the only humanist who loved, or was loved by an ill-smelling mob. The apprentices remembered him.

After the May Day episode More went to the continent on another diplomatic mission, still for the merchants, to preserve their trading privileges in Flanders. While he was gone, the "sweating sickness" broke out in England, and the King fled to Abingdon to be far from its London stench. When More returned from the continent he also went to Abingdon, for the King's call on him had become peremptory and could not be disobeyed. He had consented to enter the King's service on the condition that he should continue in it only as long as he could in good conscience. The King had been glad to accede to such a condition. Even as a boy of eight he had known More, the humanist, and because More had been the admiration of his childhood's tutor, he had imbibed with his letters a child's awe and respect for him. So he preached to More a sermon, "that in all his doings and affairs touching the King, he should respect and regard God, and afterward the King his master." These words which time has tinged with irony, were not at all ironic in Henry's mouth, nor even hypocritical. They were quite in keeping with the part that the young King was playing: that of a King who had first been destined (while his elder brother was alive) for the Church, and who had therefore a right to be more pious than most Kings. These words were neither ironic, nor perfunctory. More referred to them in after times as if the King must remember them. Nor were they spoken, I believe, simply to beguile More into the royal service. They were friendly words of a friendly King, who really understood some of More's scruples at entering his service, and who respected him not so much as a lawyer as an international humanist.

More listened to this sermon, took it indeed as a pact between the two, and trusting it, or trying to trust it, entered upon a quite different life from what he had hitherto experienced, or had ever wished for. It was not at first at all a glorious life. He could not at one wink of his eye put on the mien of a courtier, and was accordingly by the lower court officials somewhat looked down upon. They tried to impose on him, diverted the provisions of meat that were due him, and trusted that because of his unpretentious ways and known abstemiousness he would not complain. He certainly did complain. He sent word to Wolsey, that marvellous administrator, and after that what was due to him came to him. And his first occupation was not a very courtly one. It was the cleaning up of Oxford after the plague, the seeing that houses infected were properly marked, and that those who cared for the sick should carry white wands in order that they should be avoided, and, I hope, respected. But although More did not the first day begin to look like a courtier, he was now definitely at the court, and would be there ten years. A place had been found for him in the Privy Council as Master of Requests. He accepted the King's pension of £100 a year, and resigned his London office of Under-sheriff.

More disliked court life simply because it was court life. Any court demands a certain amount of flattery from its courtiers and More was second-best at flattery. As he said once of stupid flatterers who surpassed him in their art, he did not at all mind being out-run by a horse, but he resented being out-distanced by an ass. And then he definitely preferred family-life to court-life, and from family-life he was now being deprived. The Privy Council as a whole may have enjoyed considerable liberty, but there were four of the council who had to stay with the King almost as a permanent guard. More was of that four. And, further than that, he was the one man to whom the King formed a permanent attachment. The King delighted in More's conversation, liked to argue with him about theology, liked to listen to More explain about the stars, about the movements of the planets, as they walked together on the palace roof. The King so clung to More, and More so longed for Chelsea, that sometimes this unwilling courtier made himself dull on purpose so that the King would dismiss him for a while, and enable him to enjoy his day-off with his wife and daughters in relaxation by the Thames.

But also the policies of this particular court were not all to his liking. Of the internal policy he had little to complain. Cardinal Wolsey was a remarkably efficient man, who could do in one day what most people could do in two. He put an end to much of the thievery and murder which More had talked about in the Utopia. Also he was a friend to the poor, and for that reason, as well as for his arrogance, he was disliked by the great nobles and land-owners, who termed him derisively, what he may not have strictly been, the son of a butcher.

The justice of his courts was not bought justice.
But the foreign policy of Wolsey made More secretly groan for its folly, and its expensiveness had
also its evil effect at home: it impoverished the
realm.

Henry at this time was more busy diverting himself than in ruling. He was so tireless a huntsman
that his Secretary Pace said that he turned his
riding from a pastime into a martyrdom by never
ceasing from it, so he left to Wolsey the planning of
international schemes, and gave to that chancellor
a chance to play a game far above his powers. The
game was this — to make himself, England, and
England's king too, supreme. On the continent
there were two warring kings: Francis I, King of
France, Charles V, Holy Roman Emperor. So
evenly matched were they in their wars, so liable
was first one to be victorious, then the other, that
England's alliance could always turn the scale, and
was therefore sought by both monarchs. This was
pleasing to Wolsey. It enabled him to play a not
glorious, but almighty part. It gave him a chance
to assume a papal grandeur as a mediator. And,
most important of all, he from his lofty eminence
might at any moment really step into the Papal
Chair. So he continued to keep alive the conflict
between the rival kings, for its protraction, though
it might mean the destruction of Christendom,
meant for him personally power.

in the Utopia, tried to be as wise as he could even at that Tudor's court! Some of his labors were mere drab routine, the writing of letters from the Court to Wolsey; the attendance to mere papery detail. No wonder Erasmus pitied him! "And he that did this" wrote Erasmus "would, I am perfectly sure, much rather have a good laugh, than be occupied in things of Court, no matter how high they are."

More was also speech-maker on great occasions. It was quite appropriate that in 1519 he it was who made the Latin address to Cardinal Campeggio, who came, legate from the Pope, begging that England aid Christendom against the common foe, the Turk. Four years later he was the orator when London greeted the Emperor Charles V. On this latter occasion he won from the city a vote: "It is agreed that Sir Thomas More, under-treasurer of England, for his labor and pain that he took for the City in making of a preposition at the coming and Receiving of the Emperor's grace into this City shall have towards a gown of velvet forty-one shillings."

He also could guide the intellectual life of the nation. The King of England's court had at this time, like other courts, tried to become a centre of learning and letters. Henry himself was something of a scholar, and he liked to employ scholars. Pace and Tunstall, two secretarial priests of his, were excellent Greek scholars. With More now at the court, the court was with the exception of London, the Greek centre of England, more distinguished than Oxford or Cambridge. It pleased the King to think of himself as a patron of classical culture. It was one of the ways that the Renaissance kings liked to shine.

Shortly after More had joined the court, when it was at Abingdon, there broke out on its very threshold, at Oxford, a quarrel between those friendly to Greek studies and those suspicious of them. At Cambridge the great Bishop of Rochester, Fisher, was protecting the study of Greek, and as a man of piety, his patronage was respected. At Oxford a less distinguished, less pious, less learned man, Bishop Fox of Winchester had become the promoter of Greek letters by establishing his college of Corpus Christi, at which John Clements, a member of More's household, and future husband to More's ward Margery Giggs, had become recently the professor of Greek. This college came to be attacked by the teachers of the other colleges for its new and so-called "poetical" curriculum.

At the King's suggestion More stepped into the quarrel. He wrote a letter to the University of Oxford, which is remarkable not because it defends the study of Greek, — that would be expected — but because it does not assume the arrogance of

most of the Grecians. Erasmus in his saner moments had said of the scholastic dialecticians:
"I do not condemn those pursuits of theirs, except
when those pursuits are isolated." More took a
similar stand. Here is a translated part of the
original Latin letter:

"Although no one denies that a man may be
saved without a knowledge of Latin and Greek
or of any literature at all, yet learning, yea, even
worldly learning as he calls it" (More is referring
to a certain preacher whose impudence was more
evident than his culture), "prepares the mind for
virtue. Everyone knows that the attainment of
this learning is almost the only reason why students
flock to Oxford. But as for rude and unlettered
virtue, every honest woman can teach it to her
children quite well at home. Moreover, it must
be remembered that not all who come to you, come
for the study of theology. The State needs men
learned in the law. A knowledge of human affairs,
too, must be acquired, which is so useful even to
a theologian, that without it he may perhaps sing
pleasantly to himself, but will certainly not sing
agreeably to the people. And this knowledge can
nowhere be drawn so abundantly as from the
poets, orators, and historians. There are even some
who make the knowledge of things natural a road
to heavenly contemplation, and so pass from philosophy and the natural arts — which this man

condemns under the general name of worldly literature — to theology, despoiling the women of Egypt
to adorn the queen. And as regards theology itself, which alone he seems to approve, if indeed
he approves even that, I do not see how he can
attain it without the knowledge of languages,
either Hebrew, Greek or Latin; unless, indeed, the
easy-going fellow thinks that sufficient books on
the subject have been written in English. Or perhaps he thinks that the whole of theology is com-
prised within the limits of those questions on which
such as he are always disputing, for the knowledge
of which I confess that little enough Latin is
wanted. But to confine theology, the august queen
of heaven, within such narrow limits would be not
only iniquitous but impious. For does not theology
also dwell in the Sacred Scriptures, and did not it
thence make its way to the cells of all the ancient
Holy Fathers, Augustine, I mean, Jerome, Cyprian, Ambrose, Chrysostom, Cyril, Gregory and
others of the same class, with whom the study of
theology made its abode for more than a thousand
years after the Passion of Christ before more trivial
questions arose? And if any ignorant man boasts
that he understands the works of these Fathers
without a thorough knowledge of the language in
which he wrote, he will have to boast a long time
before scholars will believe him."

In this controversy More had played the part of

the sane humanist, and as sanity brings peace, so
he had played the part of the peacemaker. As
such he was recognized by both Universities: Oxford elected him High Steward in 1524, and Cambridge in the next year. Shortly after the skirmish
at Oxford More played the peacemaker in a similar quarrel. This time it was between two men,
both of them friends to More: Edward Lee, and
Erasmus. Lee was a family friend of More's. He
was a churchman, afterwards to be Archbishop of
York. When More, a young man, had translated
"The Life of John Picus, Erle of Myrandula, a
great Lorde of Italy, an excellent connyng man
in all sciences" (for so went the black-letter title)
he dedicated it to his "right entirely beloved sister
in Christ Joyeuce Leigh," a Poor Clare. Now Edward Lee was a brother of this Poor Clare, and he
was a man both of piety, and learning. He was a
friend of More's. This made the situation all the
more difficult when Lee, then at the University of
Louvain, attacked Erasmus for that humanist's
Annotations upon the New Testament, and when
Erasmus who was vain, and also older than Lee,
became at the words of what he called the upstart
greatly incensed. More stepped in between the two.
He frankly defended Erasmus, yet expressed his esteem for Lee. With neither did his friendship break
(which speaks well for Lee as well as for More), and
after it was all over More could write to Lee:

"You ask me, my dear Lee, not to lessen my affection for you in any way. Trust me, good Lee, I shall not. Although in this case my sympathies are with the party which you are attacking, yet I trust that you will withdraw your troops from the siege with perfect safety. I shall ever love you, and I am proud that my love is so highly valued by you."

More had also to play his part as the King's ambassador, sometimes in negotiations which had an aim not in accord with his wishes. He played this part loyally and skilfully: — loyally we can say, because he showed himself worthy to be trusted again and again, and skilfully too, as we can say, both for the same reason, and also because he was praised by foreign diplomats, and finally even by himself. On one of More's missions he met at Bruges one of those pioneers in European diplomacy, a Venetian, Gasparo Contarini, Patriarch of Venice, who was the ambassador of Charles V. This Venetian can vouch for one diplomatic excellence of More, namely that of keeping one's mouth discreetly and graciously shut. He had hoped to find out all about King Henry's projects from More, by talking with him when he was off his guard. "I invited," he says, "an English gentleman, Master Thomas More, a very learned man, to dine with me." That gentleman accepted the invitation, dined, I hope, well, but never to that Venetian, as the Venetian acknowledged, gave "the slightest hint" of the King's mind.

The success in diplomacy of which More himself boasted was the Treaty of Cambrai, in 1529. He boasted about it, as we shall see, in his epitaph, not, to be sure, mentioning so much his skill in helping negotiate it, as his satisfaction in having by it secured peace. Yet it must have taken some skill to secure such a peace. The wars between Charles V and Francis I had during ten years but aggravated the causes of discord. There had been two great events during the endless campaigns, the battle of Pavia, at which a French King had been made captive and led to Spain, and then two years later, 1527, the sack of Rome by the hired soldiers, Lutherans and cut-throat Spaniards, of Charles V. At the time of the first event Wolsey was the ally of Charles. At the time of the second event he had been Francis's ally. Both events Wolsey had used to stir up further rancors.

By 1528, Wolsey had so many tempests about him, that he could not keep his feet in them. Particularly the merchants were indignant against him for having endangered their trade with Flanders by quarrelling with the sovereign of Flanders, Charles V. So he tried to make a general peace, and to bring it to pass he sent to Cambrai Tunstall, Bishop of London, and Sir Thomas More. They helped make a creditable peace, fair both to

Charles and to Francis, and unexpectedly advantageous to the English merchants. More's home-return was therefore a great triumph, and he himself was willing to rejoice in it. He had done one diplomatic deed of which he in every way could be proud.

More's career then as a member of the Privy Council won for him the King's approval, and Wolsey's approval. In spite of his individual ways of doing things, the worth of his ways was appreciated, and he received constant and gradual promotion. He had begun as Master of Requests. In 1521 he had become Under-treasurer, and had been knighted. In 1525 he was made Chancellor of the Duchy of Lancaster. In 1529 he was the most practised and astute envoy to send to mend Europe's disputes at Cambrai.

Only once was there a halt in his career, — or rather what seemed to be a halt, — and the story of that halt redounds to More's honor. Parliament met in 1523, after not having met for eight years. The cause of the lapse had been Wolsey's fear of the Parliament's desire to lay hands on the riches of the clergy, and also his general liking to get along without parliaments. Men who are efficient as Wolsey was, are impatient of the palaver of parliaments, and do not like to waste their time in being politic with them. But so much money had been poured into foreign bribery, into subsidies for

other country's armies, and into the expensive
maintenance of useless expeditionary forces, that
Parliament now had to be called for the sup-
plying of money which Wolsey did not dare to
extort. So Parliament was called. It met, and More
was elected the Speaker of its House of Commons.
He who was in the King's service, now saw that he
was in the service of Parliament also, and fearing
that he might seem disloyal to one or the other, he
asked to be allowed not to accept such an office; he
was, he said, "unmeet" for it.

Wolsey interposed. The King knew More's
"wit, learning, and discretion to be such as he
might well bear the office," and the King was sure
the Commons could choose no one "meeter."
Again More accepted the inevitable honor, or
rather inevitable burden, but in accepting it he
made his position quite clear. He addressed to the
King a "humble intercession," as he called it, in
which he pleaded for two privileges: one for his
private self and the other for the whole assembly of
the Commons. For himself he asked that if by any
mishap he should, in bringing messages from the
Commons to the King, impair the wise instructions
which the Commons had given him, he should be
pardoned for any such error, and the error be im-
puted to his simpleness, and that he be allowed to
return to the Commons, confer with them, and
rectify his utterance. For the Commons he asked

— what he saw they would need — freedom of
speech. What had hitherto been but a vague and
customary right he wished to have by royal consent
confirmed. He explained to the King tactfully that
certain timorous spirits might not dare to express
their opinion honestly and according to conscience
for fear of the King's displeasure. After all, if the
members displeased the King, it must not be im-
puted to their lack of loyalty to him, nor to any
lack of desire to profit the realm, but to clumsiness
of expression, for which they should not be called
to account. Thus in accepting the speakership
More made various stipulations which have their
part in the history of English liberties.

What More feared, indeed came to pass. Cardinal Wolsey who had called Parliament for one
purpose, that it give the subsidy necessary for his
schemes, grew impatient with Parliament, when it
hesitated, and, knowing that where he stood present he often had his way, asked that he be permitted to enter the gathering of the Commons. The
Commons thereupon had a debate as to whether
they should permit him to enter alone with a few of
his Lords, or with his whole more-than-royal ret-
inue. Most of the Commoners were for receiving
him almost alone, but More remarked ironically
that it was just as well to let him come in with all
his crowd. If afterwards he should charge the Commoners for their lightness of tongue, the Com-

moners could say it was partly due to the presence
of all those outsiders. More's suggestion carried the
day. The Cardinal was invited with all the pomp he
could bring.

The Cardinal entered. The Cardinal announced
what he wanted, or what he said the King wanted,
and explained very solemnly how necessary it was
that what he wanted should be granted. He waited
for the Commoners to express their opinions. Not a
word. Then, forgetting parliamentary procedure,
for which he had contempt, he addressed individu-
ally various members to drag from them a statement of opinion. Still not an answer. At this he
recalled that possibly it was customary for Parliament to speak through its Speaker. He turned to
Master Speaker, Sir Thomas More, asked him for a
reply. Thomas More went down on his knees with
due courtesy, apologized for the silence of the
house, and explained that as for himself, in the Cardinal's presence he felt too abashed to speak. Unless all the other members should give him their
brains, he wouldn't know what to say.

Wolsey departed, angry. When next in his palace
of Whitehall he encountered Thomas More, he kept
his dignity but remarked: "Would God, you had
been at Rome, Master More, when I made you
speaker." "Your Grace not offended, so would I
too, my Lord," answered More, and looking about
the palace he began to remark, as if the affair was

forgotten, how much better he liked this gallery, that stairway, that carving, than what the Cardinal had in his other palace at Hampton Court. More did not want to prolong any quarrel with Wolsey. He did not want to start any quarrel at all. What he had done he had done because it was forced on him, and because in the end it would lead to least trouble in the world. More, by his ready tongue forestalled, outwitted, and befriended. This tongue of his, and his faithfulness to duty, won for him a position at the Court, and throughout the country, which an ambitious man might well envy. He had not so much become absorbed into the court, as he had conquered it.

But More did not, for all that, become wed to the Temporalty. The mere working for a thing often awakes our affection for it. Many a churchman, for instance, who had labored for long years in the King's service, became so interested in the well-working of its organization, that when he returned to some spiritual office, like a bishopric, his heart was still with the Temporalty. But More had no such routine affection. He kept himself detached from the Temporalty, mistrusted it.

One reason for this was its pretense. Never has the show of kingship flourished as it did at this time. It was one perpetual pageant as if heaven had come down to earth. And the pageant was hollow, for although the trappings were those which belong

to chivalry, the heart of chivalry was gone. War
was a sordid business, in which knighthood had
been replaced by paid mercenaries. Only the language of old wars continued. There is nothing that
symbolizes the false pretense of the period more
than the famous pageant of the Field of Cloth of
Gold. In the Spring of 1520 acres of sandy land
near Calais were covered with a city of gold cloth,
in which King Henry would entertain and outdaz-
zle the French King. — The only practical aim for
such a display was the making or preserving of
peace between Henry and Francis, but such an aim
existed only as pure fraud and fooled nobody, least
of all the two monarchs, each of whom was preparing for war, and knew that the other knew that he
was preparing for war. The most that can be said
for this royal pageantry was that there was a boy-
ish lavishness about it. It was a magnificent
showing-off.

Showing-off was one of the things which More
had almost too much aversion for. In the "Utopia"
the little school-children would laugh their heads
off at the foreign ambassadors who arrived all at-
tired in gold chains and decorations. The Utopia
had been written before More had entered court,
four years before the Field of Cloth of Gold, and
now More was walking around in an unbelievable
exaggeration of what he had described and sati-
rized. At that dazzling field of fraud More was pres-

ent. He was a negotiator. It is significant, however, that nobody ever thinks of him as a splendor among its splendors.

More feared the Temporalty also because he saw its tremendous power. He saw that its law of expediency was replacing the Christian unwritten law of Christendom. There had been talk in the Utopia about princes, neighbor to Utopia, far, far away, who thought they were a law to themselves. It was wiser to refer to them as far away when they happened to be so near. They were a new type of king; they were everywhere; and More feared what their wilfulness might do. No wonder, when he quitted the Chancellorship, he gave advice to Cromwell that has been remembered, namely that Cromwell should teach the King what he should do, not what he could. Any man who was a law to himself was to More abhorrent: he was a tyrant.

And finally besides having a suspicion of all tyrants, More had a suspicion of this particular, and in many ways lovable, one: Henry VIII. That superficially attractive monarch used sometimes to visit More at Chelsea and walk in More's garden with his arm over More's shoulder, — a singular and flattering piece of familiarity. Once More's son-in-law, Roper, after one of these occasions of a royal visit, exclaimed: "Sir, how happy are you whom the king has so familiarly entertained." The father-in-law answered that he thanked God for

such a master, but he added: "Howbeit, son Roper,
I may tell thee I have no cause to be proud thereof;
for if my head could win him a castle in France,"
(for then was there war between France and us) "it
should not fail to serve his turn."

Chapter VI

MORE AND THE SPIRITUALTY

While Thomas More was being drawn into higher and higher station in the Temporalty, he remained what he had always been in the Spiritualty, one of the "sancta plebs," a happy, carefree, plebeian. The Spiritualty was not something for him to rise in, but to enjoy: to enjoy first of all in the highest sense as a school which would prepare him for the examination of Judgment Day, so that he could pass it. It was enjoyable because it led to ultimate joy. But even now, in this world, it was enjoyable. It gave a sense of security. It was security. It kept men brothers, made them affable one with another.

It is many generations now since men have been talking about and looking back to, an England, a lost England, "Merrie England." In that England people wore gay colors, they danced, they sang "hey nonney, nonney," as we only make ourselves fools when we try to sing it. There may be conceivably some economic historians who imagine that England was "Merrie England" simply because the poor had enough to eat, and because

fields and cities were lovelier than they are now.
People really do not dance merely because they
have enough potatoes. They dance because God
has given them enough potatoes. If God-less
Russia became well-fed, it would not thereby become Merrie Russia, but merely well-fed Russia.
"Merrie England" was merry because it had a
sense of security, at times often even a too great
sense of security, and it derived that sense from
the Spiritualty, a government which could not
fall no matter what were the shortcomings of its
officials. Trust in the Spiritualty made peasants
dance. It made intellectuals dance, too; — the
former with their legs, the latter with their
thoughts. It gave More a freedom to laugh even at
good things: (such could not be shaken). It was
the cause of all revelry, even of too much revelry.
It gave to Wolsey his too-long train of velvetted
followers, his self-indulgence, but also, too, his
death-bed repentance.

In our day when too often we look for our sense
of security to the police power of a national government, or to the stability of the banking system, it
is very easy to mis-read the motives of those who
lived in the days when the Spiritualty was supreme.
There are conscientious scholars who pore over the
pages of the Utopia looking for what More has to
say about the clergy, and if they find a gibe here,
they assume that he was then against the Spirit-

ualty. Or they study his life and finding that two
years later he was arguing a case for the Pope,
they conclude that he had changed and was on the
side of the Spiritualty. More never expected to be
so tracked. He would have been as unprepared to
answer the question: are you for or against the
Spiritualty? as we should be by the question: are
you for or against the Universe? The Spiritualty
was one of God's ways of doing things. Of course
its members ought to be holier. Of course they
might become holier. But on the other hand they
might become even worse; and even if they did the
Spiritualty would go on. Even when it was at its
lowest ebb it was infinitely better than no Spiritualty. It was literally the source of our joy here on
earth.

It was also the source of our jests. If More had
thought the Spiritualty was a mere human thing,
he would have been solicitous about it. He would
never have allowed Erasmus to write under his
roof "The Praise of Folly." He would never have
been care-free enough to write, — even while he
was thinking of becoming a Carthusian — a Latin
poem telling of how some sailors, storm-tossed in a
foundering ship, had lightened and saved that
ship by confessing the weight of their sins to a
friar and then thrown him with that weight into
the sea. He had told the story without the slightest
suspicion that ever anybody reading it in a be-

nighted nineteenth century, could imagine that
by such a quip he was mocking at the sacrament
of penance or advising the suppression of friars.
Fortunately More could not foresee our mis-
comprehensions. Otherwise he would have practised the solemn dullness for which we have a right
to be so famous.

It was during More's lifetime that the sense of
security due to the Spiritualty, due to the confidence in its divine mission, began to fade. As a
result he saw a change in the spiritual climate of
Europe which can be compared to the physical
transformation which would take place were the
average temperature to drop ten degrees. More
thus lived in two Europes, in two Christendoms.
In the first the Spiritualty was not at all in danger.
In the second it was. And the first was a thousand
times the merrier.

None of us have seen an appreciable change of
physical climate in a country. It is not conceivable
that such a thing could take place without the
occurrence of a great cataclysm. If Florida and
Cuba dropped into the ocean, the Gulf Stream
might become seriously diverted and Labrador
seals swim round the Scilly Isles. To have changed
the spiritual climate of Christendom we assume,
therefore, that there must have been a similar
cataclysm, and by custom, and, perhaps by logic,
our attention has fastened on an event which took

place in Germany the year after More had written his Utopia: in the fall of that year, at Hallowe'en, in Germany, when Martin Luther, an Augustinian friar, posted on a church-door a paper listing ninety-five theses which he was prepared to defend — an act, which even granting that some of the theses were false, was superficially the most common-place and customary thing a theologian could do. That act, however, did lead to the disclosing of the fact that many people in Germany and elsewhere had lost that calm sense of security which the Church gives. They wanted a different kind of security, one more emotional, one that they could feel. Luther could not have destroyed Germany's confidence in the Church, but laying hands on that confidence and watching it tumble, he disclosed how rotten it had grown.

And more important he supplanted that lost confidence by a new kind of confidence taught by his manner, and by the tone of his voice. Luther as a monk — or rather as a kind of friar which is usually called monk — had been bothered by a sense of insecurity. He had become so perturbed at asking himself whether or not he would be saved in the next world, that he had tried to gain a feeling of security by ill-advised asceticism which had rasped his disposition without leading him to anything better than discouragement. To free himself from his scrupulous nervousness, and to make himself

confident in something, he took that road to freedom which dynamite follows: explosion. In other
words he cast off restraint, let himself go, enjoyed
the pleasure of giving vent to his feelings. It was to
Luther a tremendous exhilaration so to expand, to
be free, to be alone, dependent on nothing and
nobody, beyond logic, beyond thought, beyond
law, beyond your neighbors, alone with God,
ultimately, incurably saved. What an inebriating
emotion! And to many who looked on it suggested
a new sense of security: one much more inviting
than the more humble, more social, and much
more calm sense of security given to people such
as Thomas More by the Spiritualty. In fact it
laid on those who wished to enjoy it but one
serious obligation: that of discrediting all outside spiritual authority (which had hitherto been
thought necessary, but now could be dispensed
with); an obligation most easily fulfilled simply
by deriding the evil lives of the clergy who mani-
fested such an authority.

It had never occurred to Luther when he made
his outburst that he was trying to destroy the
Church, or to erect anything in its place. He still
had his respect for its priesthood, its sacraments,
and for its divine mission. If left to himself he
would, after his outburst had subsided, have
calmed down. In 1519 he was able still to write to
the Pope:

"Before God and all his creatures, I bear testimony that I neither did desire, nor do desire to touch or by intrigue undermine the authority of the Roman Church and that of your holiness." But by this time he had too great a following, some of it with no religious motive whatsoever, yet with an uncanny theological understanding that Luther was fighting the battle of the Temporalty against the Spiritualty and would deliver the riches of the Church into its hands; some of it with a craving for religious emotion. The entire following admired him for his defiance, and in order to remain their hero, there was a temptation to continue to be defiant. Hearing soon after that his books might be condemned by the Papacy, he wrote: "Let her condemn and burn my books; I, in turn, unless I can find no fire, will condemn and publicly burn the whole pontifical law, that swamp of heresies." In July 1520 he was excommunicated. Soon after that he was known even in England not as a quarreller within the Church but as a heresiarch.

On the twelfth of May 1521 Luther's books were burned publicly in St. Paul's churchyard, an act which announced England's repudiation of them. It was a gesture not of the Spiritualty alone, but of both Church and State. The Lord Chancellor, Cardinal Wolsey, who represented both, sat enthroned at the occasion. And not only were bishops and

abbots present, but also officials of the Temporalty
and foreign ambassadors. Conspicuous among
those ambassadors was the ambassador of Charles
V, in whose dominions Lutheranism was becoming
not only a religious but a grave political problem.
There were many present who were so used to having temporal affairs clothe themselves in religious
garb, that they undoubtedly thought it was a political act on Wolsey's part of amity toward Charles
V. A few may have taken it as a religious affair, but
the affair to their mind had to do with Germany
not England. There was one man, however, who, at
least, took it for what it was. That was the orator
of the day, Bishop Fisher of Rochester, of all the
bishops of England the one who united most sig-
nally learning and piety, the man with the poorest
bishopric, and the richest spiritual treasures. He
was genuinely disquieted about this Lutheranism.
He knew the faults of the clergy, and he had ten
years before this prophesied woes and persecution
for the Church, and he prayed that the Church
might be firm when the woes came. The woes had
come. He now preached a long theological sermon
in English. Most of the crowd had deaf ears. It was
an age for eyes rather than ears, eyes for pageantry,
eyes for gorgeous Wolsey on his throne. The King
admired the speech, however, for its literary excellence, and in order that it might be embalmed as a
classic had it translated into Latin.

Later on in the same year Henry finished a book of his own, which attacked Luther's doctrines, and defended the Seven Sacraments of the Church. Fisher has been accused of having written part of the book. More acknowledged that he did some collating and proof reading for it. But it was Henry's book. Henry thought of it as his own for it was his own zeal that had set him to writing it, and the orthodoxy which it contained was what he wished to stand for. As he had won glory dressed as a knight in tournament, so would he now win glory as a theologian. He would receive a title like to that of the King of France, who was called "Most Christian" or like to that of King of Aragon called "Catholic," for which title he had several times applied, thinking himself as much the most christian and exemplary of his compeers. The Pope awarded the title, calling him Defender of the Faith. And he had defended the faith; although not because he considered the faith in danger. Henry identified himself with the Church. He had been destined at first by his father to be a churchman, and counted himself therefore as almost Archbishop of Canterbury. He had never found himself in opposition to the Spiritualty. He owed his throne — he said to More — partly to the Papacy, and truly after all the Church in England was becoming a very useful tool in his hand. He really thought of himself as a very important defender of the faith. The faith could not be in danger while he defended it.

Luther read the King's book, and to give himself eloquence and confidence, fell into a fury. He called Henry a nit that had not yet turned into a louse, he called him hog's excrement, and said that he should be thrown on the "Thomistical dung-hill." Since to such an attack Henry could not with dignity reply, More, of the Privy Council, was asked to take up the defence of the King. He did it under an assumed name, and in the feigned voice of a fictitious traveller, named Rosseus. It is not the most typical work of More. It was neither humanistic Latin wit, nor English prose. It descended too near to the indecorousness of Luther. But even then it showed More, the clear thinker, defending the primacy of the Roman Pontiff, both theologically as something that should be, and historically as something which had been. He made some shrewd observations:

"I am moved to obedience to that See not only by what learned and holy men have written, but by this fact especially, that we shall find, that on the one hand every enemy of the Christian faith makes war on that See, and that, on the other hand, no one has ever declared himself an enemy of that See who has not shortly after shown most evidently that he was the enemy of the Christian religion."

He showed himself also to be a true reformer, a

man of patience: "It is far more to be wished that
God may raise up such Popes as befit the Christian
cause and the dignity of the Apostolic office: men
who despising riches and honour, will care only for
heaven, will promote piety in the people, will bring
about peace, and exercise the authority they have
received from God against the 'satraps and mighty
hunters of the world,' excommunicating and giving over to Satan both those who invade the terri-
tories of others, and those who oppress their own.
With one or two such Popes the Christian world
would soon perceive how much preferable it is that
the papacy should be reformed than abrogated."
He looked to the Pope as the one who could cure
and control Europe.

And he treated Luther not only as a personal
assailant of his King, but as an actor in the whole
drama of mankind:

"You are nothing else, Luther, but the scourge
of God, to the great gain of that See, and to your
own great loss."

This letter of Rosseus was written in 1523.
Lutheranism was treated by Rosseus as a plague
which was raging in Germany, not in England, but
already the bishops had become disturbed that
some of the students of Oxford and Cambridge
were taking an interest in the new doctrines. To an
aged man like Archbishop Warham this was very
discouraging, but it merely meant to him that

young men are always light-headed for novelty.
He blamed the infection on the new generation.
There was something in what he said. It was
natural that the young students should turn their
curiosity towards an intellectual novelty, but, besides that, the disrepute into which scholastic
philosophy had fallen, the complaints which were
being made against it by the humanists, had at
this time done much to unsettle and bewilder the
young clerics. Humanism, if they were religiously
inclined, did not satisfy them, and for logic they
had learned to have a distaste.

Then among the younger clergy there were a
few signs of Luther's seed falling on ground that
lay as if specially prepared for it. In the year 1519
there had been ordained priest in the diocese of the
Bishop of Ely, a young man of Cambridge University named Thomas Bilney. He was so small
that he was called "Little Bilney," and so timorous
that when he read in the Bible that Our Lord said
that you should go into your room and close the
door when you prayed, he could from then on pray
happily only in his room, and had to keep feeling
the door to see that it was locked. He was terribly
in dread of the Judgment Day, fretful about what
he should or should not do, and without any
masculine aptitude for logic or speculation. He
was, in short, such a man as was surely laughed at
when he should have been pitied, and who, though

he may have thought too much about himself, has
been credited by his Protestant biographers with
thinking also about others: visiting the sick and
those in prisons. In 1524 Bilney heard a priest,
Hugh Latimer, preach a sermon at Cambridge
University, which assailed Lutheranism, and, with
an audacity which had not always been his, he
went to call on Latimer, — so says Latimer himself — and expostulated, declaring that whereas
he had once been miserable now he was happy,
free from anxieties, confident of eternal salvation,
he had become a Lutheran.

Latimer followed the example of Bilney, and so
did another acquaintance of Bilney's, Barnes, the
Augustinian friar, but there is no indication that
they had the same temperamental attraction to it
as had he, for whereas he had not enough self-
confidence, they had too much of it. They represented that self-assertive wing of the Lutheranizers, who were not so much drawn to Luther by
his doctrines of salvation by faith, as by the independence in interpreting the scriptures which
his revolt promised them. To this wing belonged
William Tyndale, a priest and Greek scholar in the
West, and Frith a student at Cardinal's College,
Oxford, the latter of whom had a truculence and
love of danger quite different from the hesitancy of
Bilney and his like.

And a few laymen were beginning to be heard of

as Lutherans. They were usually of the lower merchant class, and had for trade-reasons to be very
secret about their Lutheranism, for the populace,
although jealous of the clergy's wealth and immunities, had a horror of heresy and would boycott
them. Yet although these merchants were generally
a timid, calculating lot, Lutheranism had for them
an attraction that hard liquor has for some dour
people. Possibly they saw the Church with its laws
against usury as a restraint of trade, and turned to
Lutheranism for that profitable reason, but more
often the pull toward Lutheranism was less material. It gave them the sense of being in on a secret.
It flattered their seriousness. It flattered their intelligence. They had the credulity of people who
read above their depth. Pamphlets and the gossip
of the German merchants of the steel-yard made
them think they possessed a knowledge lacking to
the priests.

A man named Humphrey Monmouth was a merchant of this Lutheranizing type. It was he who at
Bishop Tunstall's suggestion helped Tyndale to
keep alive in London, paying him, while Tyndale
was translating the Bible, his board and the not
very great price of £10 a year. Monmouth never
became an out-and-out Lutheran, not even secretly. He was knighted ultimately by the King,
and died without incurring the disfavor of that
Defender of the Faith. Yet his will shows a puri-

tanizing tendency. He forbade church-bells at his
funeral, and gave money for the preaching of thirty
sermons, rather than the singing of thirty masses,
for the repose of his soul.

But what does all this amount to? This hand-
ful of university men, these new-rich, new-lettered
crotchety merchants! Whatever we may think of
them now, they were thought of by sane people at
that day as so many cranks. And the bishops
treated them as such. In 1525 when Bilney must
have been known to be Lutheranizing, his bishop
gave him license to preach. What harm could the
poor boy do? He talked some sense among his
nonsense, and the sense could be counted on to last,
and the nonsense would be forgotten. A year later
he had become so indiscreet that he was brought
before Wolsey who treated him with the greatest
lenience, allowed him to recant without the usual
procedure, and to secure his freedom merely by
making some humble promises. A similar case was
that of Tyndale. He in 1522 had been accused of
heresy, but had been let off without being even
asked to abjure. What was he but a cantankerous
nature? Frith of the Cardinal's own college at
Oxford was accused of heresy in 1528. Wolsey imprisoned him, but let him off as soon as possible,
whence he could escape to Germany. Barnes alone
had much affair made of him, but he was an
Augustinian prior, and his importance made his

revolt too conspicuous to be passed over. It was evident, moreover, that he knew very well what he was doing. Barnes and four German merchants were made in 1526 to carry each a fagot and throw it on a bonfire in front of the road of the north-door of St. Paul's Cathedral, London, as a symbol of their recantation of Lutheran heresy. It was a solemn occasion: the Cardinal was there, and six and thirty abbots; and Bishop Fisher of Rochester preached a sermon. But the reconciliation was over and well-finished. Wolsey has been called indifferent to the spread of heresy. He was not. He simply could not think of these heretics as dangerous, not before his omnipotence.

The danger of the Lutheran heresy, however, was brought home to that other Thomas, — not Wolsey, but Thomas More — in a very intimate way, a way which made him, at least, feel the opposite of omnipotent. In 1521, the year in which More had been knighted, his favorite daughter Margaret had married a young man called William Roper. This young man has left to the world a book for which he shall ever be loved: "The Mirror of Virtue in Worldly Greatness, or The Life of Sir Thomas More, Knight sometime Lord Chancellor of England." He was loved by his wife, loved by his father-in-law. He had a temptation, however, to be overzealous in spiritual affairs, to copy the fasting and prayers of saints concerning whom he

voraciously read, but after whom he was not meant
literally to follow. The poor boy wearied himself
out with asceticism after asceticism. Then in despair and exhaustion of spirit he came upon
Luther's books "De Libertate Christiana" and
"De Captivitate Babylonica." They gave him a
sudden exhilaration. He could now dispense with
good works, and with the Church, its priests, its
pilgrimages. He walked on air, and was for speaking everywhere his new find, and for giving even of
his lands for the promotion of it. This was indeed
bringing home to More the contagiousness of
Lutheranism. It was a blow at the peace of the
More household.

More had respect for logic. He had a professional
confidence in himself as a logician. So he argued
with his son-in-law. All to no purpose! The failure
was humbling and eye-opening, and exasperating
too. Yet Roper, as he said, never saw his father-
in-law in a fume. More took it all gaily as he could,
and was infinitely patient and to the boy, himself,
loving. It was difficult, however, to keep Roper out
of the hands of the law, for he had the itch to speak
on street-corners, and he had the courage for that
too. He was in fact called to be tried, together with
Barnes and the German merchants, in that heresy
case of which I have spoken, and he would have
been tried, and he would have been forced to carry
his fagot in St. Paul's Churchyard with the others,

had not More done what he hated to do: ask for special and personal favors. He begged Wolsey to scratch Roper's name from the list.

But More had learned how little was his own power. Said he to Meg, his daughter, Roper's wife: "Meg, I have borne a long time with thy husband; I have reasoned and argued with him in these points of religion, and still given to him my poor fatherly counsel, but I perceive none of all this able to call him home; and, therefore, Meg, I will no longer dispute with him, but will clean give him over and get me to God and pray for him." Soon after he had begun these special prayers, Roper returned to the Catholic faith: its humility, its peace. More's household resumed its laughter.

In another way More learned at first-hand about the heretics. The prelate with whom More at this time was most intimate was Cuthbert Tunstall who in 1520 had been made Bishop of London. More had been on embassies with him. He had known him as a fellow-Grecian. He had won Tunstall's high respect: Tunstall had dedicated to More his most important work, one on mathematics. More's esteem for Tunstall is shown by what More said of him in the Utopia: "But of this man's praise I will say nothing, not because I do fear that small credence shall be given to the testimony that cometh out of a friend's mouth, but because his virtue and learning be greater and of more excellency, than that I am able to praise them." More was therefore near enough to Tunstall to be well-acquainted with Tunstall's troubles, and Tunstall had his troubles, for by being made Bishop of London, he was made supervisor of that district where heresy found it most easy to propagate.

More heard from him that these Lutheran zealots, if few, were difficult to deal with. In the first place they were enthusiasts. They could not be silenced. If they abjured their heresy, as almost all of them were ready to do in these early days of the 1520's, their abjuration amounted to nothing. Their promises to be obedient or to keep their thoughts to themselves, were promises to which they never felt themselves bound. These men could always by their vehemence convince themselves that they were right no matter what they did. Also they were not dullards. Claiming of course that they were not heretics, they tried to teach their doctrines as if they were teaching what had always been taught. They inserted into books, which were known to be orthodox, little additions that appeared harmless, because allied with the good. They spread new versions of the Seven Penitential Psalms with nothing lacking in them other than the litanies and dirges which had been invariably associated with them. This was as much as to say, "You do not have to call upon the saints any more. You do not have to pray for the repose of your father's soul." And also they were setting about to translate the Holy Scriptures, adroitly insinuating into the English versions phrases which seemed literally correct enough, but which skilfully hinted new interpretations. At this last device Tyndale was the great artist.

Tyndale, of whom I have already spoken as being a priest from the West of England, was later tobe called by More "the Captain of English heretics." He was certainly already the chief thorn in the side of Tunstall. He was not by temperament at all like Luther. Luther was a beer-drinker, he could be boisterously affable. Tyndale had a sour nature. When he was in Gloucestershire, tutor to the children of a man called Walsh, he had such a sharp, discontented look that neighbors did not like to dine any more with their friend Walsh. Neither did Tyndale have the nervous inquietudes of Luther, nor the thirst for Luther's doctrines of faith. In fact he showed signs of becoming heretical after his own manner, not in Luther's. It was his hatred of scholastic philosophy, a hatred learned by him at Oxford from John Colet, which had inclined him to a new theology founded on a literal interpretation of the Bible. He believed that, no matter how ignorant you were, you could interpret the Bible for yourself. The Holy Ghost would see to it that you made no mistake. — That is, you could interpret the Bible correctly if

you were to be saved. Otherwise you were lost.
Like Luther he had little sympathy for "the lost."

Tyndale was a good Latin and Greek scholar.
He was an earnest man, a courageous man, in
some ways uncannily sagacious, but he was really
quite incapable of understanding people other than
himself. This led him to disappointment after disappointment. In 1523 he came to London, and had
letters to Bishop Tunstall. He took it for granted
that because Tunstall liked Latin and Greek letters, because Tunstall liked Colet — then more
than ten years in his grave — he and Tunstall
must therefore be kindred spirits looking at everything alike. He was grievously disappointed that
Tunstall did not like his cure-all. Tunstall did not
treat him, however, at all as an enemy to the
Church. On the contrary he helped him, but was
suspicious of him, and secured for him no great
benefice or funds. He knew that Tyndale was translating the New Testament, and liked the idea in itself. Yet was Tyndale wholly to be trusted? Tyndale went on working in his chagrin, — one against
the world. Then an Oxford man named Frith came
to talk with disappointed Tyndale. They discussed
Luther, became not Lutherans, but friendly to
Luther. Tyndale, bent on saving the world by his
translation of the New Testament, went to Germany. They might take him more seriously there.

In 1526 there began to trickle into England Tyn-

dale's Testament, — although it was not at first
known to be Tyndale's. The Bishops could not
help seeing the Lutheran bias to the choice of
words in the translation, but Cardinal Wolsey with
a certain contempt for mere words, thought that
even then nothing should be done about it. Let
it circulate. Yet it was on second thought condemned and burned. Such an act could no longer
suppress a book. The printing press was making
it possible for a book to be in a thousand places
at the same time. A printed book could be almost
God-like, infinitely multiplied. It was all very well
for Bishop Fisher to write against and confute in
learned Latin the not-too-consistent doctrines of
Luther, but the battle was now being carried on
elsewhere, in the English-reading public, among
London citizens, among unprofessional theologians.
Tunstall's enemies were in that field employing
a new kind of eloquence, whose power was not
logic, but vehemence. It had absolute conviction
behind it, fiery fervor copied from the Hebrew
prophets. More described the Lutherans in England as a "few malicious mischievous persons."
So they were. But they were unassailable, uncon-
trollable. They had to be met with their own
weapons, or own weapon; English eloquence. Tunstall and the bishops called upon More as an orator, a poet, a theologian to come to the aid of the
Spiritualty against these new foes.

More might have bowed had he been addressed as an orator or as a poet, but the title theologian he would not claim for himself. He was a mere layman like his neighbors. Moreover he, since he had first been able to hold a pen, had made mock of those who tried to be what they weren't. As a youth of twenty he had written:

> When a hatter
> Will go smatter
>   In philosophy,
> Or a pedlar
> Wax a meddler
>   In theology,
> All that ensue
> Such craftes new
>   They drive so far a cast
> That ever more
> They do therefore
>   Beshrew themselves at last.

Yet More could not help seeing that the Spiritualty did need his help at this time. A bishop who spoke against heresy might be suspected of leading a skirmish in the growing war between the Spiritualty and the Temporalty, and might draw to the aid of the heretics some who were merely jealous of the Church's power. Or if a scholastic theologian spoke — a Dominican for instance — he might in defending the Church against heresy, awaken the antagonism of the young humanists who disliked his logic and provoke an alliance between Lutherans and humanists. More was not an officer in the Spiritualty. On the contrary he was an officer in the Temporalty, and therefore his act of defending the Church could not be taken as an incident in the conflict of Church and State. And neither was he a scholastic theologian. He was a loyal layman and a humanist. Who, when he spoke, had a better chance to be listened to and not to be misunderstood, than he?

And what a privilege he had too as a layman! This modern theological quarrel was not a learned Latin one. It had descended to the popular plane of the vernacular, to which the clerics were not used. It had also taken on a manner abusive and rude, like that of a street-fight, from which the dignity of priesthood had to keep itself aloof. More had no such aloofness, no such dignity to guard. He could mingle in the tumult, talking as man to man. He could tell merry jests, befriend, mock, cajole, be in fact direct and rude as a London lawyer, and yet, with all that, companionable.

More was a layman in the true sense, not in the twisted sense the word has acquired in the unfortunate quarrels of France. Laymen in France, and in other countries too, during the last few centuries, have been taken to mean men as opposed to priests; men as outside the Church. Laymen are laymen, and were originally called laymen precisely because they were a part of the Church. More was a layman, which meant that he was loyal to his Church, and he accepted the invitation of Bishop Tunstall. He championed the Church, and allowed himself to be called by the Church's enemies "the bishop's proctor."

Chapter VII

THE CHURCH'S CHAMPION

From now on for six years More was to stand
out as the champion in England of the Church,
its defender against the heretics. He was to take
up his pen when he was a busy member of the
Privy Council. He was not to put it down until he
had become a member of that group of either
famous or notorious Englishmen who have lodged
in the Tower of London, with a not-inviting destiny ahead of them. When he wrote his first words
he was in good health. When he wrote his last,
he had a cramp in his side, and was broken in
strength, largely through having written too much
when he had already too many other things to
do.

His chief opponents were two priests and two
lawyers: the priests, Tyndale and Frith (with
whom might be included Friar Barnes); the
lawyers, Simon Fish and Christopher Saint-
German. What he talked about with these men
wandered from legal affairs — had such and
such a heretic been rightly treated according to
the laws of the land? — through statistics about

the wealth of the clergy, to matters of pure theology — what is the Blessed Eucharist? — But More saw that in all this controversy there was much talk but only one real question: Which was the Church, Tyndale's Congregation, or the Church with the Pope at its head which Tyndale called a fraud? More kept to the central issue.

It is not my purpose at this very late date to rise up, and defend More, proving that he was right, as if no one had done it before, but the world has not yet grown tired, — nor will it soon tire, — of remarking the unique quality of More as a controversialist: his own quality. He was Thomas More in it from beginning to end, and his defense of the Church reveals as well as does all his life a trait in him which marks all he was or touched. It is a trait which showed itself when he entered into the revels at Cardinal Morton's Court, and which did not leave him on the scaffold, when he was to die. It went up on the stage of death with him, and prompted his jests and kiss to the executioner. It can be described by a word which I would apply to it if the word had not been contaminated by parlors and too much talk, and which even then I do apply to it: sociability.

More's sociability harks back to the beautiful origin of that word, rather than to any of its unfortunate significances here and there. It showed when he did noble things, as when he treated other men as if they had a right to exist, when he addressed them as if they had a right to be considered reasonable beings, when he jested with his adversaries, when he assailed them not mincingly, when he assumed a tone of companionship with them from which he would not depart, when he repudiated even the shadow of self-righteousness. And he was sociable also — as is less often observed — in his habit of putting forward those doctrines which unite men, rather than those which separate them.

More's first controversial work did not preach a sermon. It talked, it conversed, man to man. Its first endeavor was to make its readers feel at home. It was a dialogue — called usually "The Dialogue. Quoth I and Quoth he." — in which a pleasant fiction enlivened and charmed many a reader, but certainly not Tyndale who mocked at the fiction as "feigned poetry." — A messenger was invented, or drawn from real life, who came to More to ask More questions which others who sent him had wanted him to ask, questions about these so-called new doctrines, and their promulgators. — Were they as dangerous as made out? — More writes an account of his imaginary conversation with the messenger, just as he had written of his imaginary conversation with Hythloday in the Utopia. There was no feud to recount therefore. The Messenger was regaled. He was even dined.

More discussed with the messenger questions which More, who was ear to the talk of the town, knew to be the talk of the town. They had a practical bearing. They were: first, had the Spiritualty done wrong in making a certain young man abjure (the young man Bilney)? Second, was it right to burn and condemn Tyndale's Testament? Third, what harm was there in Luther and his sect? Fourth, is it fair to war against infidels and put heretics to death?

The scrupulous Bilney had taught — so More said, and so all agreed — that "we should do no worship to any images, nor pray to any saints, or go on pilgrimages." Such teachings were heretical. Why? Were they contrary to the Scriptures? Yes, they were, explained More, but the Scriptures were not the Church. They could not speak out. They had to be read and understood. They had — in order to be absolutely trusted — to be interpreted by a voice which could not err: the Church's. So far, so good. Even the Lutherans were in accord. Of course the Church could not err. But what was the Church?

Indeed what was the Church? The messenger had heard the new definitions of what it was. Might not Luther's followers be the Church? Where were they yesterday? asked More. Or per-

haps only those Catholics who are good, — or
who think themselves good — are the Church?
"No," said More in his great catholicity. "The
Church must needs be the common known multitude of Christian men, good and bad together,
while the Church is here in earth. For this net of
Christ hath for the while good fishes and bad."

This unsanctimonious, unselfrighteous, un-
pharisaical view of the Church made More not a
tense purist who thinks that there are no abuses in
the Church. I might say, if I were not sure that
I should be misunderstood, that More was glad
that there were abuses in it. It reminded him that
he was human, and what a thing — human nature
— it was that Our Lord came down to assume, and
out of which God was constructing a Church. Men
of the type of Bilney were terribly upset by the
human nature which showed itself still human even
on pilgrimages, and were therefore in favor of
suppressing pilgrimages. Pilgrims not only often
misbehaved like some of Chaucer's Canterbury
pilgrims, but they were overcredulous of, over-
eager for too-frequent, or grotesque miracles. More
laughed at the squeamishness that took at such
things offense. When told by the messenger that
there was a saint in the North of England, Saint
Uncumber, to whom wives prayed that they might
be freed from their bothersome husbands, even by
the death of those husbands, — Think of that! —

More's only rejoinder was to inquire if he was quite sure they were not praying for their own death to free their husbands. And as for miracles, if it came to telling absurd miracle-stories, he could tell a better tale than the messenger. Had the messenger ever heard of the bishop who in the building of his church found one beam cut a great deal too short for his work, and drew it forth — he and another man pulling against each other — to a full four feet longer than it was, and made it serve? — How about that for a good miracle story! —

But if the Church had its very, very human side, it had also its divine side. More was not one of those who are content with the human merely because it is human. He saw the grandeur of pilgrimages. And the miracles which so often gave their approval to pilgrimages were not all feigned miracles. He described reverently one of which he had first-hand knowledge:

"And as for the point that we spake of concerning miracles done in our days at divers images where these pilgrimages be, yet could I tell you some such done as openly, so far from all cause of suspicion, and thereto testified in such sufficient wise that he might seem almost mad that hearing the whole matter will mistrust the miracles. Among which I durst boldly tell you for one, the wonderful work of God that was within those few years wrought in the house of a right worshipful knight

Sir Roger Wentworth, upon divers of his children, and specially one of his daughters, a very fair young gentlewoman of twelve years of age, in marvellous manner vexed and tormented by our ghostly enemy the devil, her mind alienated and raving with despising and blasphemy of God and hatred of all hallowed things, with knowledge and perceiving of the hallowed from the unhallowed, all were she nothing warned thereof. And after that moved in her own mind and monished by the will of God to go to Our Lady of Ipswich. In the way of which pilgrimage, she prophesied and told many things done and said at the same time in other places, which were proved true, and many things, said lying in her trance, of such wisdom and learning that right cunning men highly marvelled to hear of so young an unlearned maiden, when herself wist not what she said, such things uttered and spoken, as well learned men might have missed with long study, and finally being brought and laid before the image of Our Blessed Lady, was there in the sight of many worshipful people so grievously tormented, and in face, eyes, look and countenance so grisly changed, with her mouth drawn aside, and her eyes laid out upon her cheeks, that it was a terrible sight to behold.

"And after many marvellous things, at the same time showed upon divers persons by the devil through God's sufferance, as well all the remnant

as the maiden herself in the presence of all the
company restored to their good state perfectly
cured and suddenly.

"And in this matter no pretext of begging, no
suspicion of feigning, no possibility of counterfeit-
ing, no simpleness in the seers [i.e. onlookers] her
father and mother right honorable and rich, sore
abashed to see such chances in their children, the
witnesses great number, and many of great worship, wisdom, and good experience, the maid herself too young to feign, and the fashion itself too
strange for any man to fain. And the end of the
matter virtuous, the virgin so moved in her mind
with the miracle, that she forthwith, for aught her
father could do, forsook the world and professed
religion in a very good and godly company at the
Minoresses where she hath lived well and graciously ever since."

The second question, which concerned the condemnation and burning of Tyndale's Bible gave a
chance to More to explain even further his
conception — the Catholic conception — of the
Church, this time in regard to the relation of
clergy to laity. Of course, More believed that
translated Bibles were good things. He made that
clear, and he made it clear that his view was that
of the clergy also. But the translations must be
devoutly and carefully made. Tyndale's Bible is
maliciously translated. — Where? More cites a

dozen places, of which take one. Where priests of the Jews or of Baal are spoken of, they are translated priests especially where they were scolded. Where Christian priests are mentioned they are spoken of as seniors, — a word says More not even of our language. — The reason for this was obvious. Tyndale wished to do away with priesthood.

Priesthood! At this the messenger tried to turn aside into one of those self-satisfying luxuries: a diatribe against the faults of the clergy. More cut the ground from under him by quoting his friend Colet (whose fault-finding with the clergy the heretics liked to quote themselves). Colet had said that if the clergy be nought, the laity must needs be worse. More did not expect the miracle, that all priests should be good. He was quite ready to acknowledge, — in fact he suggested, — that there were too many priests, for men without vocation were being ordained, yet the habit of the heretics in finding nothing but faults in the clergy, was their own heretic-fault. They were like vultures who never look at live sheep, only at dead carrion. And although he did not rebuke the messenger, he hinted something to him with the remark that whereas most men think that the only shrew in the world is their wife, they would do better to think that the only worthless person in the world was their own self.

More did not like Tyndale. He did not consider

him straightforward. But against Luther he had a
much deeper antagonism. This was not merely
because Luther was his most important adversary,
the instigator of the entire heretical movement,
nor was it because Luther had shocked him — as
he had indeed — by his act which turned More's
throat dry with horror, the marrying of a nun.
Nor was it only that Luther was to his mind definitely a heretic, a man who had wilfully committed
a sin of changing Christ's doctrines, than which
— More said definitely — there was no sin more
displeasing to God. But the very heresies which he
chose were those such as More found it the most
easy to detest. More and Luther were such different men.

Luther liked to push himself forward, More
to step back. Luther was hasty, unsteady, More
deliberate. Luther was explosive, More calm.
Luther shouted, More liked a low voice. And
spiritually they faced opposite ways. More liked
to take into account — he enjoyed taking into
account — those about him, above him, beneath
him. He liked to be dependent on them. Not so
Luther. More quotes with detestation what Luther
had said: "I care not for Augustine. I care not
for a hundred Cyprians, I care not for a thousand
Jeromes, I care not but for scripture alone, and
that is plain on my part." More perceived that
Luther could not abide "the common anthem of

Our Lady, the most devout Salve Regina" because in it Our Lady is called Our Advocate.
More, on the other hand, liked that prayer for the
very reason that it gave him an advocate. And
in what possible connection or circumstance can
we imagine More referring to himself as Luther
referred to himself: "The man of God, Luther?"

As More ran to doctrines which united men,
Luther ran to their opposite which divided men,
and since Luther made a religion for himself out
of the doctrines to which he ran, it was only natural that More and Luther ended up worlds beyond
worlds apart. More was for sociability, Luther was
for what, if you feel complimentary, you can call
individualism. Take for instance Luther's doctrine
of salvation by faith alone, a doctrine which, to
use More's phrase, spiced all of Luther's doctrines. By such a doctrine a man was exempt in
his spiritual life from having anything to do with
material things. He lost a companionship with
holy images, holy water, sacramentals in general.
He became very much like a pure spirit which unfortunately we are not. And less social than that,
a man by Luther's doctrine became, no matter
how companionable he might be with others in
purely temporal affairs, not companionable with
them in spiritual matters. In other words he was
not dependent on anyone but himself.

Not only did Luther's teaching separate man

from man, but it cleft the individual man: his reason from his faith, grace from nature. More naturally abhorred the teachings of Luther, as teachings which tore apart. When the messenger, therefore, asked More if Luther's writings did not contain so much good that the bad could be overlooked, More did not have to strain himself to answer that Luther's writings were like wine containing more than half poison. And then as if that simile were not strong enough he added that even the wine had been turned by the poison rotten.

More regarded Luther's changes in doctrine as dangerous not only to the ultimate safety of every individual soul touched by them, but also to the safety of society on this earth. He foresaw as logical consequences to Lutheranism public calamities not all of which came as soon as he expected, but whose arrival he thought he saw indicated in two events which occurred before he wrote "The Dialogue": the bloody insurrection of the German peasants, and their bloodier suppression, and the desecration and sack of Rome by the half-Lutheran Imperial army.

When More went on to discuss the treatment of heretics, these social consequences of Lutheranism were always in his mind. Even those whom I call heretics agreed with More that the sin of heresy was a great one. The question put to More by the messenger was as to whether or not it was charita-

ble to lay violent hands on heretics. Should they
not be left to themselves and to God? More's
answer was that the temporal princes for the
sake of temporal society were forced to lay violent
hands on heretics who were themselves wielders of
violence. Otherwise, anarchy, like the peasant revolt, and sacrilege, like the desecration of Rome,
would mar all Christendom.

At this the messenger asked if the unsocial heretics could not be peacefully by persuasion led
from their heresy and made social. Couldn't they
be reasoned into the truth? When More answered
this question he was thinking of the heretics he
knew, whose revolt was against reason, who had
exalted faith to the exclusion of reason, and therefore by their principles were unreasonable, or un-
reasoning. How then treat them as amenable to
reason? They were deaf when you argued with
them, mad when they spoke themselves. They
reminded him of Collins, a maniac, in the insane
hospital, Bedlam. He alone could "lash" out
Scripture like Luther and Tyndale. It was not
for the Church, the Spiritualty, to use violence,
but it was for those with authority in the Church
to identify the heretic, and then the temporal
prince had a right on the heretic to use violence.

No sooner had Tyndale seen More's "Dialogue"
than he replied to it, writing "An Answer unto
Sir Thomas More's Dialogue." In it he hurled

some hard words at More, calling him Balaam,
Pharaoh, and even Judas, and threatening him
"with vengeance of God and evil death." This was
not a sign of mere fury in Tyndale, an indulgence
in word-slinging. Tyndale felt himself right. Therefore he was right. He assumed the righteous indignation, and some of the righteous eloquence too,
of the Hebrew prophets. Therefore he was a Hebrew prophet, and More who was his enemy was
an enemy of the prophets, and worthy to be
spoken to as he spoke to him.

But aside from this exaltation Tyndale really
misunderstood More. He thought that More's liking for merry tales was a sign of frivolity. He called
More's use of make-believe, shown in the "Dialogue" as well as in the "Utopia," so much "jug-
glery" or "poetry," and because More had once
noticed that all priests were not virtuous he
thought that More must now have been bought
by the priests to be willing to defend the
Spiritualty. "But, verily, I think that as Judas
betrayed not Christ for any love that he had unto
the high priests, scribes and Pharisees, but only
to come by that wherefore he thirsted; even so
M. More (as there are tokens evident) wrote not
these books for any affection that he bare unto the
Spiritualty, or unto the opinions which he so
barely defendeth, but to obtain only that which
he was an hungered for. I pray God that he eat not

too hastily, lest he be choked at the latter end; but that he repent, and resist not the Spirit of God, which openeth light unto the world."

Tyndale's answer to More failed to be an appropriate answer first because it was addressed to an imaginary More who existed only in Tyndale's fantastic misapprehensions, but also because it was written, though in English, in another language, or better, though in the same language, on a different plane, from More's. More had tried to argue calmly, logically. Although he is not usually thought of as a Thomistic theologian, he knew St. Thomas Aquinas so well that he said when he heard the argument of some opponent of his: "That is merely the objection which Saint Thomas at such-and-such a chapter quotes in order to refute it," and he had the scholastic habit of stating his adversaries' side at length and with fairness. More clung for all his poetic leanings to a scholastic sobriety, very different from Tyndale's vehemence with its "Mark ye this" and "Mark ye that," which made More exclaim that Tyndale sounded like a scorer at tennis-play with his "Mark, mark." Thus Tyndale spent his force trying to move people, More in trying to convince them by logic.

It is interesting to note also that when they jested, they jested for a different purpose. Tyndale was not given to jesting, but when More had developed at serious length the Catholic doctrine concerning the various kinds of devotion — latria, dulia, hyperdulia, — and concerning what kind of devotion was due to sacred images and relics, Tyndale broke in with the gibe: which kind of devotion was it that More paid to a Cardinal's hat? Now, it is not because it was disrespectful that I single out this jest as something different from what More practiced. More, himself, made jests about the Lutherans which to them may have seemed equally disrespectful, as when he listed the wives, so hastily married by the Lutheran leaders, as being the only theologians whose authority they could cite. But the guffaw which Tyndale's jest raised gave Tyndale a chance to escape from the necessity of having to discuss soberly the question of the various kinds of devotion. It enabled him to go on referring to a respect for images as idolatry. It was a deliberate evasion, and no doubt to his audience an effective one.

More, on the other hand, never used his jests to free himself from intellectual effort. He used his jests after the combat was over to befriend the very enemies he had made, or during the combat as illustrations of the argument which he was putting forth. And he used them when he was bluntly disagreeing with an opponent not so much to make fun of his opponent as to make fun of himself and of all of us. Luther, for instance, said there was no use in confessing to a priest. If you wanted to, confess to a friend, a man or a woman. This gave More a chance to laugh about how difficult it is for some of us seeing a group of priests to choose one in seven years to whom we should like to confess, but now that a fair woman can hear confessions, it will be easy for us to confess once a week.

But in spite of the misunderstandings between More and Tyndale, in spite of their failure to fight on the same field, they did on one thing agree: namely, their difference of opinion about what was the Church. Tyndale was never ready quite to forget eloquence but he did define his Church as "the whole multitude of all repenting sinners that believe in Christ, and put all their trust and confidence in the mercy of God; feeling in their hearts that God for Christ's sake loveth them, and will be, or rather is, merciful to them, and forgiveth them also all the motions unto sin, of which they fear lest they should thereby be drawn into sin again." Such a Church was like More's in that it could not err — according to Tyndale — in its teachings. Its definition had a similar sound, also, because of its Christian phraseology. But its differences from More's were greater than small words can express. All the people in it were good, and knew they were good. They knew they were saved. They were sure to be saved. They were secret. They were a Church Invisible — each man, and each man only, knowing his own membership in it. It was exclusive. It was a little flock. Said Tyndale significantly: "God reserved him a little flock ever in Israel, and had ever prophets there, sometimes openly, and sometimes in persecution, that every man must hide himself, and keep his faith secret." It was, in other words, just the opposite from the Church Catholic. Its very mark, — sanctimoniousness — is that which the Catholic Church is marked by not having. It was just such a Church as More's sociability would have shrunk from with horror.

After Tyndale had written his "Answer to Sir Thomas More's Dialogue," More replied to it with his "Confutation" and later with his "Apology." Of these the "Confutation" has often been derided, — and was derided by Tyndale — for its length. The length of it, nine books, such as would take up three quarto volumes, is indeed tedious, but it attests to the scrupulousness of More in wishing to be thorough. He himself defended the length saying first that he was not surprised that Tyndale had found the book long, for Tyndale had found other things too long: notably the rosary by all of its "Hail Mary's." And he added: "It is a shorter thing and sooner done to write heresies than to answer them." But, more important, he explained that much of the length was due to his care to quote Tyndale, his adversary, in his fullness, and not to quote him as Tyndale quoted More, that is "faintly and falsely" and leaving out "the pith and strength" and "proof" of More's arguments. With excellent courtesy the Protestant editor of Tyndale's Works, the Reverend Henry Walter, representing The Parker Society, has, writing as far back as 1850, corroborated More's own statement concerning his fairness to Tyndale. He says: "It is however to the credit of More's fairness, as a controversialist, that the extracts from Tyndale incorporated into his Confutation are so many, and so accurate as to have been of material use to the present editor in his endeavor to form a correct text."

The "Apology" is not merely a continuation of the "Confutation," and like the "Confutation" only a further discussion of questions raised in the "Dialogue." Other opponents had entered into the controversy, other questions also. Perhaps most important was the question of More's own conduct: how just had More been as Lord Chancellor, how merciful to heretics? Because that question was and is important, the discussion of the "Apology" falls into that chapter which later shall consider Thomas More as he appeared in that high office. But here and now can be mentioned and should be mentioned his reply — so late and so patient and so affable — to Tyndale's charge that he had been bribed to defend the Spiritualty.

More acknowledged that some of the bishops had raised for him a collection: five thousand pounds. He had refused their offer. His answer to them had been laconic: how could they imagine he was either so virtuous or so unavaricious of spare time as to be willing to put himself to such labor for so paltry a sum?

While More was in controversy with Tyndale and in that controversy was showing himself sociable, jealously sociable, with all living men, he was in another controversy showing himself sociable with the dead, the dead in Purgatory, who needed his prayers. This new controversy was conducted with an enemy to whom he felt more friendly than to Tyndale. The enemy was a layman, Simon Fish, a lawyer, who had acted in a satirical interlude at Lincoln's Inn, which mocked at Wolsey. In dread of Wolsey's indignation, Simon Fish had fled to the continent, and there, himself in high indignation against Wolsey, had written a book, which very likely some discontents of a more theological bent had persuaded him to write, and for which they gave him information and misinformation. The book was called "The Supplication of Beggars," and was the work of a young man, who gave not two thoughts to any theological doctrine, but many thoughts to getting revenge on Wolsey, and on the clergy. He suggested that the riches of the Church be taken away and given to beggars. Then there would be no poverty. Suppress, he urged, particularly the endowed chantries which pray for the souls in Purgatory. Purgatory, he had been told, does not exist. It is very expensive. Forget about Purgatory.

More responded to Fish's book with a book of his own appearing under an opposing title: "The Supplication of Souls," in which the souls in Purgatory plead their own cause. In defending the souls he was not neglecting the beggars. It is safe to say that he had a deeper pity for the beggars and the unemployed than had Fish. He had shown his sympathy by not being able to keep from pleading for the beggars in his "Utopia." But that did not prevent him from seeing what was in the mind of Simon Fish. He told Fish that such a cure-all as robbing the Church had been sophistically and maliciously conceived, — yes maliciously, although he hoped and prayed that the young man who had practiced that malice would repent and return to the faith — which he did. More showed the faulty information written and garbled by Fish. He showed how the Church was not so wealthy as was made out. And finally he showed that there was a Purgatory, and that souls in Purgatory no more than earthly beggars should be forgotten. They were both neighbors. He pleaded for the souls in Purgatory, or rather allowed those souls to plead for themselves, begging our prayers, especially our great prayer, the Mass:

"If ye believe our need and care not for us, alas, you lack of pity. For whoso pitieth not us, who can he pity? If ye pity the poor, there is none so poor as we, that have not a bratte (i.e. rag) to put on our backs. If you pity the blind there is none so blind as we, which are here in the dark, saving for sights unpleasant and loathsome till some confort come. If you pity the lame there is none so lame as we, that neither can creep one foot out of the fire, nor have one hand at liberty to defend our face from the flame. Finally if you pity any man in pain, never knew ye pain comparable to ours whose fire so far passeth in heate, all the fires that ever burned upon earth, as the hottest of all those passeth a feigned fire painted on a wall."

And then the soul ends up:

"Remember our thirst while ye sit and drink, our hunger while ye be feasting, our restless watch while ye be sleeping, our sore and grievous pain while ye be playing: our hot burning fire while ye be in pleasure and sporting; so might God help you hence, or not long here, but bring you shortly to that bliss to which our Lord's love help you to bring us, and we shall set hand to help you thither to us."

Scarcely had More finished with Fish than he had to answer another lawyer, this one not driven by private spite, but animated by a theory. The man's name was Christopher Saint-German. Because of all the opponents of More he was the one who is by fame the worst treated, let us say what good can be said of him. He was less of a theologian even than Fish, but he was more of a lawyer. He was a lawyer with a hobby, which was a desire to see the jurisdiction of the Church much diminished, and the common law extended to the exclusion of canon law. He did not think of himself as an enemy of the Church. He was so blind to things spiritual that he really did not know that he was acting as an enemy of the Church. Very probably without instigation from the King he would never have entered into written controversy at all. He would have merely bored his neighbors by his talk, and continued to collect, what he had, a large library. And finally in the books which he did so bothersomely write: first "A Treatise Concerning the Division between the Spiritualty and Temporalty," and then "Salem and Bizance," he did show a legal acumen which made him one of the few men of the time who saw the logical consequences of their theories, and yet were not afraid to be theorists. He saw for instance that the road which Henry was travelling towards making himself, a King, master of the Church, would in the end lead to having Parliament legislate God's law, — and he personally thought that a good road.

Where Saint-German was foolish was not in such reasoning, but in calling himself a Pacifier. He was a poor blind bookworm of a mole, come out into the day of public life, and dazzled thereby when he pictured himself as a friend to both Temporalty and Spiritualty, as one to be welcomed as such. He was no such thing. He was so partisan against the Church, so credulous of "some-says" against it — to use More's expression — so prejudiced in his legal statement of the case that More had to devote half his "Apology" and a whole book called mock-heroically "The Debellation of Salem and Bizance" to refuting him. So absurd was his pretense at peace-making that More likened him to a man who seeing a Procession of the Blessed Sacrament passing through the streets and being attacked by heretics, should for the sake of impartiality enter into the fray himself, reviling and rebuking the priests, "or at leastwise some of them" and "sowsing them in the mire."

Christopher Saint-German was not a Lutheran. He had no interest whatsoever in such doctrines as justification by faith. Neither was he wilfully a stirrer-up of discord. He wanted peace, but peace with the Temporalty supreme. He wished for an accord between men, based on their natural interests. His heart and treasure were with the Common Law. All of which merely brings out his difference from that other lawyer, Thomas

More, who looked for peace from a different quarter, from above rather than from below, and who considered that the true bond of unity was a spiritual bond, and that its permanence depended on a due respect for the Spiritualty.

In other words as distinguished from Saint-German's conception of sociability, More's was a supernatural one, which assumed the supernatural and could not exist without it, which looked to God, and not except in its proper place and for what it could give, to Parliament. To define even more clearly More's spiritual conception of unity there came his controversy with a priest called Frith. Frith was an adventurous spirit, an audacious one, who by his danger-loving quality has awakened among historians an admiration, which has called him the most charming of the Lutheranizers in England. He had dared become Lutheran before Tyndale, and had been forced to flee, and had been allowed to flee, to Germany. There he had married, and thence he had returned to England at the downfall of Wolsey, thinking that a golden era for heresy had arrived, only to be clapped into the Tower of London by Sir Thomas More, then Chancellor.

The Tower could not repress Frith, nor intimidate him, and, contrary to the advice of Tyndale, who counselled craft: "Creep low by the ground and follow meekness," he attacked a doc-

trine, which neither love of lucre, nor jealousy of
the clergy, nor any local spitefulness, had as yet
weaned the English people from cherishing. It
was the most intimate doctrine of Christendom.
For it cathedrals had been built, and for it towns
had crowded round cathedrals. By it Christendom
was happy and hopeful of its human nature. By
it Christendom was one. By it More could feel an
unfathomable companionship with his fellow-men,
a companionship that reached to God. To describe it Saint Thomas Aquinas had said that by
it God had approached more near to the entire
Christian people than ever to any nation. I mean
the doctrine of the Blessed Eucharist. Frith from
the Tower declared such a doctrine empty.

More answered Frith. His answer was neither
violent, nor long. Was this because he felt responsible for Frith, having put that heretic in the
Tower? Did he have a special pity for, or hope
in Frith? I believe it was rather the reverence for
the subject which kept More from raising his
voice. The devotion to the Sacrament of the
Altar was his deepest devotion. In speaking of
it he felt "the abashment of his own unworthiness." "To approach the Blessed Eucharist" —
so he said once — a man's soul in his body has
need to be "such a child in innocency as was that
infant Saint John 'who leaped in his mother's
womb for joy.'"

More who wrote the "Answer to Frith" was the More who was accustomed to say that prayer before the Blessed Eucharist which he copied down in the Tower, and which I take to be of his own wording: "Take from me good Lord this lukewarm fashion, or rather key-cold manner of meditation, and this dullness in praying unto Thee. And give me warmth, delight and quickness in thinking upon Thee; and give me Thy grace to long for Thine holy sacraments, and specially to rejoice in the presence of Thy very blessed Body (sweet Saviour Christ in the holy sacrament of the Altar) and duly to thank Thee for Thy gracious visitation therewith and at that high memorial, with tender compassion, to remember and consider Thy most bitter passion. Make us good Lord virtually participant of that holy sacrament this day, and every day make us all lively members, sweet Saviour Christ, of Thine holy mystical Body, Thy Catholic Church."

Chapter VIII

THE KING'S WILFULNESS

If the quarrel between the Church and the new Lutheran heresies had remained unobscured by other quarrels it is difficult to imagine how in England the Church would not have conquered, for where the quarrel was seen clearly as one between orthodoxy and heresy, the people were overwhelmingly for orthodoxy. But now this quarrel became obscured by another quarrel, in reality trivial, but which at that time seemed more important than this skirmish between the all-powerful Church and heresy. The new quarrel was between the King and the Pope. It had nothing to do with heresy. The King wanted but one thing: to have his way.

During the first fifteen years of King Henry's reign, his way had accorded very well with the Pope's way, which had led Europe to think of Henry as a very obedient Christian. He attended daily two Masses. Sundays he was punctilious at High Mass. He defended the clergy against a Parliament greedy to take from the clergy some of their wealth, some of their immunities. He

made the great churchman, Cardinal Wolsey, more
powerful in the kingdom than even he himself.
He discussed theology always loyally to the
Church's teachings. He wrote the not only pious
but musical hymn "O Lord, the Maker of all
thyng." He wrote even other hymns. Fourteen
years after his coronation he was so alacritous in
the defense of orthodoxy that he wrote for and
sent to the Pope, when Luther had attacked the
Papacy, his Defense of the Seven Sacraments. In
that book he had so exalted the position of the
Pope that Sir Thomas More had pointed out to
him that he may have gone too far in associating
the Spiritual Preëminence of the Pope with the
Temporal prerogatives like his prince-ship over
this or that city in Italy. Henry would not change
his words. Even in temporal quarrels where the
Pope seemed to be acting too much as a mere
Italian potentate, against Venice for instance,
Henry was careful to be the political and military
as well as the spiritual ally of the Papacy. But
Henry was not an obedient man, for an obedient
man bends his will to that of another, even when
to suffer that bending it, hurts. Henry was a
spoiled child who did not like to be hurt.

It also seemed to Europe that Henry was a
virtuous man. He was hailed as the model monarch. He could dance, he could sing. He could
play the organ. He was anxious to do things

better. He hired the organist from Saint Mark's
basilica in Venice to come to England and give him
organ lessons. He could speak Latin, French, of
course English, Spanish, Italian. And he could use
those languages, Latin for theology, French for
love letters, English for verse. What a genuine
lyrist he was!

> "O my heart, and O my heart,
> My heart is so sore."

So sang the greatest poet among English kings,
except perhaps Richard Coeur-de-lion.

And still more wonder. He was a graceful ath-
lete. He could play tennis so well that it was a marvel to watch him. He could tire out six horses. In
near-war, in tournament of make-believe knights
— not a lady-like game, — he was almost heroic,
unseating adversaries. In wrestling too he had his
prestige and his pretensions, and even though he
was thrown by the French King in their jaunty
wrestling match at the Field of Cloth of Gold, he
was able to take that defeat as a good loser. And,
then, he was a faithful husband, — at least during
the first ten years of his reign, — and after that,
when he had Elizabeth Blunt as his mistress, and
from her a child, and even when he had, in due
course of mistresses, Mary Boleyn, sister of the
future temptress Anne, he was a no more un-

faithful husband than his brother-monarchs of that day nor than many better Kings before or since.

Yet there was a deception in Henry's virtues, and in his talents, and in his first faithfulness to his wife. He liked the show of being things, rather than the being them. He liked to dress like a knight, to charge in tournament like a knight, but he was no warrior. Theology had a great charm for him. It was a game. He played it with Cardinal Wolsey arguing whether or not a layman should restrict himself to merely vocal prayer, and bored the Cardinal terribly. His faithfulness to his wife was that kind of faithfulness which keeps a man true to his wife during his twenties, and equally false and cruel to her in his thirties. He was of a disposition easily influenced, and his wife influenced him. She played the part not only of wife, but of mother to him. He took the easiest path, which was not at first wicked, for his natural inclinations were better than those of most men. He was never a strong character. He was first and last a spoiled child.

Sometimes because Henry married enough wives to do for seven men, he is pictured as a brute of lust, an animal. It was not his masculine lust which led him astray in life, it was his feminine wilfulness. He wanted his way emotionally. His first wife Catherine was the daughter of that pair of monarchs, Ferdinand and Isabella, who had sent

Columbus across the ocean and made Spain rich with America. Henry's father had sought this young girl's hand for his eldest son, Arthur. He needed the alliance of Spain and he was so anxious for the support of his own cause, that he saw to it that young Arthur was at birth engaged to be married to Catherine aged three. He also saw to it that the King of Spain, who also wanted the English alliance, and who wanted his offspring to win the world by marriages, should pay him be-loved money: one hundred thousand crowns: half the ultimate dowery. In 1501 when these children were old enough to be allowed to be married, but not old enough for Arthur to consummate the mar-riage, they were married. Shortly afterwards Ar-thur died. Because the money had, so much of it, already been paid, because the alliance with Spain was still desirable, this same Catherine was now set aside for Henry, who should be later Henry VIII, a prince who was six years younger than Catherine.

There was some difficulty in the way of Henry's marrying Catherine. After all, she was, in marrying him, going to marry the brother of the boy with whom she had at least gone through the ceremony of marriage. It looked like the marriage of a man with his brother's widow, a kind of marriage not usually allowed by the Church. To surmount this difficulty a dispensation was received from the

Pope, and the difficulty would have been, at least
for many years, forgotten, had it not come to pass
that Henry VII, when his son was old enough to
be married, was not quite so sure that he wanted
or needed Catherine for a daughter-in-law. Or was
it really that he wanted a larger dowery for her,
or the complete payment of the dowery for the
first marriage? At any rate Henry VII so long as
he was alive delayed his son's marriage, making
this excuse or that excuse for the delay, and sometimes for a diversion suggesting doubts as to the
validity which such a marriage would have.

But once Henry VII was dead, Henry VIII who
needed a wife and a queen, chose for that wife and
that queen, Catherine, his sister-in-law. He was
eighteen and handsome. She was twenty-four and
not beautiful, but the marriage does not appear
to have been contrary to the inclinations of Henry's
heart, even if it were primarily a political marriage. It had not even the incompatibility of the
usual marriages of a king with a foreign princess.
Catherine had been in England so long, she had
become English. At any rate they began to reign
together, happy as larks. Their delight in pageant
made them a delight to the entire nation. They
were good to look upon.

Even seven years after their accession they were
still the youthful pair going a-maying from Green-
wich together to high Shooter's Hill, espying there

a company of tall yeomen, clothed all in green, who pretended to be Robin Hood and his followers. They shot their arrows for the King and the Queen, — did these make-believe bandits, — and then invited the couple into the Greenwood, where under arbors they spread forth rustic fare: wine, venison. There was a high-heartedness to the marriage, which did not soon wane.

But there was also an undercurrent of tragedy. The year after the marriage Catherine gave birth to a premature child, daughter, born dead. The year after that she gave birth to a boy who lived three days. The year after that, 1513, she gave birth to another boy born dead. The year after that she was again with child. Henry was at the time very angry at her father who had made peace with France secretly and left him alone fighting France. Henry scolded Catherine for her father's conduct. Catherine was nervous about these births that were not births. The result was another son, still-born. At this Henry, who was beginning like a grown man to wonder who would come after him, became impatient. If his wife couldn't give him a child, mightn't he find a wife that could. He remembered that his father had had to get a dispensation for him to marry Catherine. Perhaps there were flaws in the dispensation. At any rate lawyers could find flaws in it. Then he would find himself unmarried. He could begin again with a new wife. Within another two years, however, a live child had been born. She was a daughter, Mary Tudor, but at least a daughter, at least an heir.

"We are both young," cried Henry, the King, in his joyousness, "if this time we have a daughter, with the grace of God sons will follow." Two years later for the last time Catherine was with child. In November 18th, 1518, the heart-breaking result was a son, a dead son. The next month Henry thinking about his one heir, that two year old daughter, engaged her to be married to the Dauphin of France who had not yet had his first birthday. This engagement did not last long, for four years later Henry was at war with France once again. But even before the engagement fell through, he saw that it did not solve the difficulties about the succession. Nobody in England wanted a French King of England. In 1521 the Duke of Buckingham, the nearest male heir to the throne, had been tried, and judicially murdered. It was said he was aspiring to the throne. Some blamed the execution on Wolsey's spite, but was it not also royal conspiracy? Clear the way for your own children. Mary was growing up. Could she, a girl, really control the nobles, Parliament, England?

Henry began to look around for a boy. It was indeed difficult to find such a thing: a boy at least that could be his legitimate heir. Catherine could give him no boy. Elizabeth Blunt, his mistress, had given him a boy, but the boy was a bastard, even though he recommended himself by resembling his father. In 1525 Henry created that child Duke of Richmond and Somerset, titles which suggested titles borne by his father, and prophesied a throne for the boy. But there are always difficulties in the path of a bastard. Would it not really be much better if he could have for himself not a new mistress, but a fresher, more fecund wife? And, besides everything else, he was becoming weary of Catherine. His appetite began to look around. Yet he still liked to think of himself as very holy.

In 1522 when war broke out between England and France there came back to England from the French Court a girl who had there learned French manners and the ways of the world: Anne Boleyn. She had beautiful long black hair and black eyes, but as for charm she had an angularity which to the French was repellent. She had even deformities, a mole on her neck which she covered with a ribbon, a defect in the fingers, sometimes referred to as a sixth finger. She may have had a secret seductiveness which could not be described, and could not by some or most even, be felt, — Wolsey called her a crow of the night — but, however that may be, she certainly did have one thing which to the emotional, uncalculating King, was a charm and a tantalization, and a trap; namely, a strong will.

Henry had seen her in 1522: she was one of the queen's ladies-in-waiting. He had also cast eyes on her, greedily. Anne, who was ambitious, was then trying to win as a husband for her ambition a youth who was learning to play the courtier at Wolsey's court. He was Percy, heir to the duchy of Northumberland. Possibly her father, who had a merchant name but was allied by marriage with the Howards, set her at this marriage. At any rate the King interfered. He sent word by Wolsey to young Percy that Percy must look elsewhere. How Anne for the next two years played with the King's appetite no one shall know. But she played with it so skilfully, that at the end of three years the King began to let fall the opinion that he had never been married at all. He had grown able even to convince himself that in living with Catherine he was living in sin, — a most extraordinary and convenient feat of the conscience. There began to be talk of an annulment of Henry's marriage.

Such talk did not greatly surprise the courts of Europe. They were even expecting to hear some such thing. But it did not occur to them that Anne Boleyn was the cause of such a plan. They never imagined that she could be ever Queen of England. They did not think that the King's

lust had anything to do with such a suggestion.
They assumed that he was being guided by foreign
policy, cold-blooded, calculating. He was aiming
at the obtaining of an heir, or at a reversal of
alliances. As for the suspicion that the King of
England had any real scruples about the validity
of his first marriage, that never touched them.
You could not have surprised Europe with such
an idea. Europe would simply not have believed it.

Cardinal Wolsey was nearer to the scene. He
knew surely that the King's longings were being
tormented by Anne Boleyn. But being quite devoid, if not of religion, at least of religiosity, he
could not imagine that the King was genuine
when he talked about scruples. What the King
was suffering from was lust for "a crow of the
night": Anne Boleyn. Lust is something which
passes or which changes its object. So Wolsey forgetting what the King's wilfulness might be, or
what a will a woman might have, imagined that
Henry would soon possess Anne, then throw her
away. But since the King had brought up the matter of annulment, he, Wolsey, might as well use
it for what it was worth. It was a card in the international game.

It happened that just at this time England's
ally Charles V had won what to Wolsey was a
too great victory over Francis I. In fact, Francis I
had been captured by Charles. Wolsey, especially

after Charles had refused to help Henry VIII to
the vacant throne of France, was bent on curbing
Charles' power, and particularly Charles' arrogance. He threatened to join France against
Charles. Especially he threatened it in a round-
about way, by suggesting that Henry would cease
to be a husband to Charles' aunt Catherine of
Aragon, and become the husband to some French
princess. Such a threat was very opportune. The
Pope Clement VII was not very robust. Perhaps,
if the Pope died, Wolsey, who had twice failed
of being elected Pope, might dicker with the Emperor, playing with this threat of a new marriage
alliance, and thus secure the Emperor's help towards climbing the Papal Chair. Playing with
the annulment might help him to his heart's
desire.

Thomas More seems to have been the one man
who saw that this idea of an annulment, which
the King was dallying with, might lead to great
harm to Christendom. More understood the wilfulness of the King, and the King's religiosity.
The King was one of those characters which want
to be right and wicked at the same time. They do
not break laws and repent. They twist laws, and
call sins virtues. They do not have to repent.
And they are dangerous to more than themselves
by the lengths they will go to justify themselves.
Said More one day walking with his son-in-law

Roper along the banks of the Thames: "Now, would to Our Lord, son Roper, upon condition that three things were well established in Christendom, I would put in a sack and here presently cast into the Thames." "What great things be those, Sir?" asked Roper. "In faith, son, they be these," said More. "The first is that whereas the most part of Christian princes be at mortal war, they were all at universal peace. The second, that where the Church of Christ is, at this present, sore afflicted with many errors and heresies, it were well settled in perfect uniformity of religion. The third, that where the matter of the King's marriage is now come in question, it were to the glory of God and quietness of all parties brought to a good conclusion."

The King's true wilfulness had not been shown in his random sayings of 1525. To become fully developed it had to be goaded by the refusal of Anne Boleyn to give herself to him without marriage, and by the sense, irritating to him, that the annulment which he wished might not be so easily attained. Before two years more were out that goading had taken place. He was frantic for Anne, and his first try for an annulment had failed.

This first try had begun and ended thus. In May 1527 Wolsey, who was throughout Europe coming to be blamed for this whole disturbance,

put on, at the King's suggestion, a show of right-
eousness, and summoned the King and Queen before him to rebuke them for having lived twenty
years together without being married. The comedy
that thus began was by Wolsey — for once a playwright — to be continued by the King confessing
his mistake, and by the Queen doing likewise.
Whereupon Wolsey, the Papal Legate, would declare that since they were not married and could
not be married, — being within forbidden degrees of relationship, — they should separate.
Catherine would no longer be queen. The Pope
would in due time confirm the decision of Wolsey.
But the Queen refused to play her part. She declared that she had never even been married to
Henry's brother-in-law, for Arthur had been too
young to consummate the marriage. She appealed
to the Pope to protect her.

This was very embarrassing to Wolsey, for it
was not a time at all to approach the Pope. The
Pope was practically a prisoner of Charles V,
whose army had captured Rome, and the Pope
could scarcely be expected at such a moment to
anger the Emperor Charles V by dissolving the
marriage of the Emperor's aunt, and by insulting
the Emperor's family. Later on the right time for
approaching the Pope might come. First peace
must be made between England and France. Then
the power of Charles V must be abased. Then,

when the Pope was free, and Charles by the turn of fortune, down instead of up, an annulment might be secured. And by that time, furthermore, Henry might be over his infatuation for Anne Boleyn, and ready to make a sane political marriage. The pause in the proceedings of an annulment was a happy one. It was time for other things.

There were nobles behind Anne Boleyn, relatives of hers, the party of the Duke of Norfolk, and others merely jealous of the upstart Cardinal, who were too impatient to think it was a time for other things. They knew nothing of diplomacy, cared not at all for theology or canon law, but they knew with all their greedy vigor, that Wolsey was cleverer than they, that he was not really their friend although he was working for an annulment as were they. They wanted Anne queen not because they were opposed to Catherine or to an alliance with the Emperor, but because they were opposed to Wolsey. They could control the King, if Anne supplanted that Cardinal. So they decided to act on their own accord, behind Wolsey's back. They had the King's support, although the King was too shamefaced to let Wolsey know that they had it. They would send their own man to Rome.

Knight, a priest, a half-blind chaplain of the King's, was the ambassador of these impatient nobles to the Pope. His instructions were folly; his execution of them was equally folly. He was told to get permission from the Pope for Henry VIII to have two wives. Didn't the King deserve it for his loyalty to the Pope, for his services to the Church? He was told also to get permission for Henry to marry as second wife a woman, even if that woman's sister had been the King's concubine — a not very hidden allusion to Anne Boleyn. — On his way through France, Wolsey who was there, absent, making peace with the French, got hold of Knight and tried to straighten him out. He put enough worldly wisdom into Knight's head to keep him from being laughed at by asking for the privilege of bigamy. He rushed to England and had the King send further instructions to Knight. Let the Pope be asked to endow Cardinal Wolsey with powers to act as if he were the Pope.

Knight found the Pope at Orvieto whither he had escaped from Rome. The Pope was not at all anxious to make Wolsey any more omnipotent than he already was, and Knight was not anxious to have the Pope so make him. Many papers were handed to Knight which he, inexperienced, scarcely understood. He thought they gave him all he asked for and as much as he needed. He sped home to England. When he arrived there and Wolsey and the canny lawyers had read the papers, it was found that the papers meant, for all their verbosity, exactly nothing: they merely al-

lowed Henry VIII to marry again if he were not
already married.

This failure may have pleased Wolsey's pride,
and may have nerved him to show what he now
himself could do. Yet it disturbed him, for what
was it but an attempt to proceed without him?
He was being supplanted. The King knew that
Wolsey would not approve of the marriage with
Anne Boleyn. (In fact Wolsey had already tried
to dissuade the King from it.) But the King was
so bent on having Anne that he would cast Wolsey
aside in order to have her. There were two paths
open to Wolsey: to oppose his desire for Anne,
or to give Henry what he desired so much, and
secure his further gratitude. He made up his mind.
He stepped in, lordly. He would straighten everything out. Of course the King's marriage must be
annulled. He pledged himself to get anything the
King might ask from the Pope. If the King wanted
Anne for queen, let him have her.

But still the Pope was in the Emperor's hands,
and besides that, the Pope had that tremendous
responsibility for representing heavenly justice
which he could not fail to feel. Would he be sure
to find the King's cause a just one? It was possible
that there were flaws in the dispensation given by
Julius II to Catherine to marry her brother-in-law.
It was possible that the King no matter how ig-
noble his motives had the legality on his side.

But no chances could be taken. The Pope must let the affair be decided in England by him acting as Pope. He flattered the Pope, therefore; showed to him how England was rescuing the Papacy, from the wicked giant Charles V. And he threatened the Pope. Let the Pope beware. Unless he gave Henry what he wanted, there would be schism in England, then heresy. Look at Germany.

The Pope gave to the King or to Wolsey much more than he wanted to give. He sent to England Cardinal Campeggio to judge, with Wolsey, the case of the marriage-annulment. He allowed, to his everlasting remorse, this Cardinal Campeggio to carry with him a bull which automatically annulled the marriage of Henry and Catherine provided Wolsey and Campeggio in their legatine court should decide that the former marriage between Arthur and Catherine had been consummated. But the bull was strangely given: it was not to be shown or entrusted to anybody. And Cardinal Campeggio should carry it very slowly, and he should try when he got to England to temporize, to allay the King's passion, to let the affair blow over, so that the bull should never have to be used.

It was not until June 21st, 1529 that the trial was called in England, and even before the trial was called Wolsey was turning white with anxiety. The Emperor had discovered in Spain a document in which Pope Julius II had given a dispensation to Catherine to marry her brother-in-law Henry even if her marriage with Arthur had been consummated. Wolsey, the Pope's Legate, could not very well say that a Pope had no right to give such a dispensation. So the trial hesitated. It was playing for time: the Pope, Clement VII, was sick. He might die. Queen Catherine after the first day, quitted with the applause of the populace (who were on her side), the court of trial. Here was a strange mix-up: the populace were angry at the Pope and at Cardinal Campeggio for just the wrong reason: they thought Campeggio was against the Queen. But the court of the Legates did not have to make time for many months. In July, Clement, who did not die, sent word to England revoking the commission of the Papal Legates, calling the case to Rome.

This brought the downfall of Wolsey. Campeggio had no troubles, except that his baggage was searched for the strange Papal Bull on his way from Dover to Calais. But Wolsey had taken the affair of the annulment out of the hands of the Duke of Norfolk. He had pledged himself to succeed at this trial. He had failed. He was now useless to the King's wilfulness. Let him be cast aside. A Bill of Indictment for Praemunire — for having exceeded the powers accorded to a repre-

sentative of the Pope by English laws in England
— was brought against him. Of course, if he had
exceeded those powers, it was not the Pope's
doing, but the King's. No matter! He was summoned to appear before the court of the King's
Bench, a lay-court, from which he was exempt.
Abject, to save his life, to try once again to win
the King's favor, he submitted to this court.

Now it was up to the nobles to get the divorce
for the King: Wolsey had failed. They had no
reverence for the Pope nor loyalty to the Pope.
They were, according to Chapuys, the Ambassador of Charles V, as Lutheran as the Lutherans, —
by which of course he did not mean that they were
worried about their salvation in the next world,
or were conceiving new formulas to define faith,
but that they were utterly contemptuous of the
Spiritualty. — If the Church in England, now
without its legate, did not of its own accord annul
the King's marriage with Catherine, they would
put the Church on the rack. They would turn the
Commons, greedy for gold, on the Church's
treasure. They would turn the Lutheran heretics
on the Church's truths. At this very instant,
Parliament after five years was being called. It
was being seen to that its members were of an
anti-clerical complexion. And Tyndale, the Lutheran, had just written a book concerning Christian obedience in which he had maintained that

blind obedience was due to temporal rulers. All allegiance was due to the King. The King should be more absolute than any Pope had ever been or thought of being over the English Church. He was its head. The untheological nobles heard of this book. They gave it to Anne Boleyn, opened at a proper page. Anne laid it in the lap of Henry, — the page not turned. "This is a book for me," exclaimed the King.

Yes, it would be easy enough to punish the Church and intimidate it. The Commons were panting for spoils. But the same Commons who were against Wolsey, against the independence of the Church, were also against Anne Boleyn. Even the Lutheranizing Germans of the Steelyard were courageous, and entitled to a salute therefor, in their loyalty, an even temerarious loyalty, to Catherine. Henry had to convince his subjects that he was really wicked in keeping Catherine as his wife, — which would be difficult. He had to make his new policy of marriage with Anne polite, palatable, and he really wanted to keep the friendship of his English clergy, even if he were willing to enslave them. He needed to have for his Chancellor a man whom all England trusted, to vouch for the nobility of his conduct.

There was one man in England whom all people did trust. The Commons had confidence in him: he was of them. The clergy had chosen him as their champion against the Lutherans: he was their friend. The nobles knew him as possessed of ability, yet not ambitious: he might be their servitor. He had already, when scarcely over fifty, become a legend. Schoolboys learned about him. In the "Vulgaria" of Robert Whittington, a book of Latin rhetoric, there was an exercise: say in four ways in Latin "More is a man of an angel's wit and singular learning"; first grammatically: "Morus est vir divini ingenii et singularis eruditionis"; then, oratorically: "Morus est vir mirando ingenio et prestantissima eruditione"; next historically: "Morus est vir preclarus ingenio et eruditione"; fourth, poetically: "Morus est vir prestans ingenii et eruditionis." This exercise since 1520 had been having its effect on the rising generation. And Thomas More — for he was the Morus and he was the man to whom I refer — was not only a legend, he was at this moment an active and living figure, crowned with a recent triumph: the Treaty of Cambrai.

In October, 1529, Wolsey fell. He had lost his footing in a storm which he did not expect, and which indeed turned everything topsy-turvy, in which friend was often fighting friend, thinking that friend his foe. The very same storm swept Thomas More into an importance, which was not of a kind warranted either by his remarkable abilities or by his equally remarkable virtues and learning. He became indispensable to the King. He was in that same October of Wolsey's fall offered the Great Seal of Lord Chancellor. He accepted it.

Chapter IX

THE KING'S CHANCELLOR

More, as Chancellor, did his best to be loyal to the King, and in order that he might feel loyal he turned his back on the ugly affair of the marriage annulment, and of the scheming of the King towards acquiring it. Not that he was at all blind to its insidiousness. Two years previous the King had asked More for his opinion on the annulment, and had opened before him the Old Testament (just as if theology were really the affair). More had pleaded that such things were over his head. Why not ask two really wise men? The King asked who they were. "Saints Jerome and Augustine," was More's answer. He wanted to leave it to the theologians. But he knew what was ever in the King's mind. He knew that he himself had been chosen to be Chancellor indirectly to further that very annulment.

He kept his eyes on affairs that were definitely his. They were not all those affairs which Wolsey, as Chancellor, had charge of. Wolsey, a single indefatigable man, the last Chancellor who was really Lord Chancellor, had been succeeded not

by one man, but by a group: Anne Boleyn, the
Duke of Norfolk and some others, the King's
Secretary, — first Gardiner then Thomas Cromwell, — still others. Only one of Wolsey's functions
fell full into More's hands: that of dispensing the
King's justice, being the Supreme Judge of the
realm. Wolsey had been a good supreme judge:
impartial, a protector of the poor. More was a
better one. He gave to justice its terrible effective-
ness: swiftness. There ran a rhyme:

> "When More some time had Chancellor been
>   No more suits did remain,
>   The same shall never more be seen
>   Till More be there again."

He also tried to temper the severity of English
Common Law, which at this time gave the death
penalty to thieves as it did to murderers. To
temper it he was excellently placed, for his code as
Lord Chancellor was neither Roman Law, nor
English Law, it was a higher equity, resembling
absolute justice, and so dependent on the Chancellor's own sense of what was fair that the measure
of the Chancellor's justice was proverbially likened
to the length of his foot. This independent position
of the Lord Chancellor had in times past brought
the Chancellor into opposition with the common
law justices. More incurred a similar opposition.
Resorted to as he was by those who somehow felt

too poor, too unimportant, to receive justice elsewhere, he took cases from under the eyes of the
other judges, who resented it. To befriend them, he
invited them to dinner, explained why he had
acted as he had, and satisfied them. In softening
the cruelty of English law, he was able to carry out
what Raphael Hythloday had recommended in
the first, — the more serious, — book of the
Utopia, and he anticipated, so the lawyers tell us,
the idea contained in the English Judicature Act
of 1873, whereby law and equity can be adminis-
tered by the same tribunal.

More had also to be, which was not so agreeable,
the mouthpiece for the King. At the opening of
Parliament in November 1529, he made a speech
in which he surely likened King Henry to a shep-
herd and pointed how a King was, and he should
be, a guardian of his people. According to Hall, the
Chronicler, he added to this a diatribe against
Wolsey in which he likened Wolsey to a wether
who "scabbily" and "craftily tricked" his shep-
herd. This does not sound like More's tone, and it
sounds very like what Hall thought about Wolsey,
so it is possible to regard the diatribe as fictitious.
But, leaving that aside, More in speaking as he did
in the King's behalf must have had to use words
which gave the impression that he sided with the
King more than he was always at heart able to.

Take for instance a speech he had to make a

month or two later. He had, at the bidding of the
King, to explain to Parliament how "the virtuous
King" doubting of the validity of his marriage had
applied to the various Universities of Europe for
their opinions, which opinions having been given,
seemed to approve of the King's doubts. "Then
Sir Brian Tuke took out of a box twelve writings
sealed, and read them word by word." — So says
Chronicler Hall. — And those opinions were from
Orleans, Paris, Angers, Bourges, Bologna, Padua,
Toulouse. These opinions were not in some in-
stances, what they pretended to be, and in all
cases they had been extorted or paid for. Padua's
opinion was worth a little over £500. — And More
knew this.

Sometimes the King had two policies: one con-
tradictory to the other: one open to the world, the
other hidden. For instance, he wished to defend
England against heresy. He genuinely wished it.
At the same time because he wished to intimidate
the clergy and force them to do what he wanted,
he was willing to encourage their enemies: the
Lutherans, whom he did not think to be really
dangerous. They might, like a mild poison, be not
harmful if taken in small potions. So he summoned
Friar Barnes and Friar Barnes' wife back to England, and gave to Friar Barnes a safe-conduct. —
Friar Barnes was a great blamer of the clergy, a
great hater of Cardinal Wolsey. — And he sent

encouragement to Simon Fish, and he invited
Christopher Saint-German to continue his writings
against the too-great powers of the Spirituality.
And he was not only for spreading Tyndale's doctrines about the supremacy of the Temporalty over
the Spiritualty, but he was for having Tyndale
back in England. He sent a messenger for him.
Unfortunately for Tyndale, Tyndale had spoiled
his own chances of return, by writing precipitately
a book against the King's divorce, thinking with
that typical Tyndale blindness that the divorce
was only a scheme of Wolsey's, which had fallen
with Wolsey's fall. Tyndale did not return. And
all this invitation to heresy was being given by a
King who really detested Luther's doctrines, and
who had just taken over the censorship of books,
because the clergy had been so helpless in prevent-
ing the spread of those which were heretical, that
he felt called on to help them.

More closed his eyes to the King's connivance
with heretics, he treated the King as if he were
heart and soul against heresy. Whenever as Lord
Chancellor he had to come upon heretics he was a
repressor of them. This does not mean that he
outran the King's real wish, or that of the people.
A hundred years before this, in 1401, the clergy and
Parliament had appealed to another Henry, —
Henry IV — to make a formal decree that heretics
should be punished by burning. Such a law had

previously been taken for granted as a part of the
Common Law of England, and a hundred years
later it had not grown repugnant either to King or
to people. More, himself, would have been quite
ready to defend its justice. Yet More wished to go
not as far as King and people might have wished
him to go. He tempered justice with mercy. His
manner of repressing heretics was first to treat
them kindly, to entertain them even as a guest in
his house, and at the end to go no further than to
make sure that they did not spread their doctrines;
to which end he would inflict imprisonment, extract promises.

He had no difficulty finding heretics. He could
hardly avoid them, for the King had taken over the
censorship of books, and the duty had devolved on
More to get information concerning heretical pub-
lications. In investigating such matters he came
across information about Thomas Philips, a
leatherseller in London, who seemed to be a
trouble-maker. He called Philips to him. In his
"Apology" he tells us what happened: "And when
I had spoken with him, and honestly entreated him
one day or twain in mine house, and laboured about
his amendment in as hearty loving manner as I
could: when I perceived finally the person such
that I could find no truth, neither in his word, nor
in his oath, and saw the likelihood that he was in
the setting forth of such heresies closely, a man

mete and likely to do many folk much harm: I by endenture delivered him to his Ordinary. And yet by for because I perceived in him a great vainglorious liking of himself, and a great spice of the same spirit of pride that I perceived in Richard Hunne when I talked with him, and feared that if he were in the bishop's prison, his ghostly enemy the devil might make him there destroy himself, and then might such a new business arise against Master Chancellor that now is, as at that time arose upon the Chancellor that was then, which thing I feared in Thomas Philips somewhat also the more, because a cousin of his, a barber in Pater Noster Row, called Holy John, after that he was suspected of heresy and spoken to thereof, fearing the shame of the world drowned himself in a well; I for these causes advised and by my means holp, that Thomas Philips (which all be it that he said the clergy loved him not seemed not yet very loth to go to the bishop's prison) was received prisoner into the Tower of London." (From More's Apology, Chap. XXXVIII.)

At least two heretics were by More's orders flogged. One of them was a child, apprenticed in More's household somewhat as More had been apprenticed in that of Cardinal Morton. The lad's father had previously had him "nursled" (to use More's phrase) by a George Gee, alias Clark, a priest who later fled to Antwerp, was there married, and who received into his house there, the two nuns which John Birt, stole out of their cloister "to make them harlots." This unsavoury priest had filled the child with "ungracious heresies" against the Blessed Sacrament of the altar, and gave the child an evil zeal to propagate those heresies among other children even in More's household. When the lad had begun on another child, More caught him at it. "Upon that point perceived" says More "I caused a servant of mine to stripe him like a child before mine household, for amendment of himself and an ensample of such other."

The other flogged heretic had a habit more shocking to some of us today. He would go into Church during Mass, wait till the reverend moment of elevation had arrived and then would steal up behind some woman deep in her meditation, and "lift up all her clothes and cast them quite over her head." More had this man flogged. "God be thanked," says More in his Apology, "I hear no harm of him now."

After More had been Chancellor for a year and a half, the King extorted from the clergy the title of Supreme Head of their Church in England. This gave the King a sense that he did not need the Lutheran help any more, and also that he must show how good an orthodox chief of the Church he was, so he himself began to be a persecutor of the heretics and a much more drastic one than More. As a result, three of them were put to death. In the previous twelve years when the clergy had had charge, not a single heretic in the diocese of London had been put to death, and the change to severity can be blamed on the King rather than on More, for More, in fact when it occurred was but waiting his opportunity to resign from the Chancellorship. When these punishments were inflicted, he was no longer even in friendship and confidence with the Bishop of London, for his friend Tunstall had been elevated to Durham, and Stokesley, a mere tool of the King's, had been set in his place. These punishments can not be attributed to More. They were Henry's.

It is often said not that More was cruel, but that he was inconsistent: When he had written the Utopia he had believed in absolute toleration; now he quite frankly did not. Those who bring such a charge should remember, first, that Utopia was not England, it was *nowhere*. It was inhabited not by Englishmen but by "philosophers." Secondly there was no such thing as absolute toleration in Utopia. The philosophers were just as intolerant as philosophers (according to More) have a right to be. They demanded that a man believe in God, and that he be not violent and bullying in whatever supernatural religion he holds to. Third: there were no heretics in Utopia. Philosophers — Aristotle,

Plato, — are not heretics. They are simply noble thinkers unillumined by grace, unaided by Revelation. Such respectable citizens inhabited Utopia. — And no intellect — it is and was a canon law of the Church — can be forced to change its mind by violence. And fourth: it must be remembered that a heretic is not one who does not agree with another, or one who is ignorant; he is one who tries to twist to private or temporary ends the Revelation given by God into the guardianship of the Church. He pretends to be a Christian, to be speaking for the Church. His offense can take place only if there is a Church, for you cannot have counterfeit money unless you have real money. And fifthly and lastly, it should be remembered that there were, — as there were not in Utopia — heretics in England. There were heretics in England, and they were almost without exception violent. God knows that More knew that many Catholic Christians in England were in most affairs utterly unreasonable. For that reason More had written the Utopia. But the heretics were a thousand times more unreasonable than the worst Catholics. They not only failed to live reasonably, but they did not believe in reason — or Luther explicitly did not.

It is not right to charge More with inconsistency. Of course heretics were more dangerous in 1530 than in 1516. Of course a man could not laugh with the same freedom, after Luther's revolt had begun.

But More's attitude toward heretics was always fundamentally the same. It was partly Christian, partly medieval, Christian in that it hated heresy, yet loved the man who held the heresy: medieval in that it believed that the Temporalty was so bound to the Spiritualty that it had a right and duty to suppress heresy. More's attitude towards heresy and heretics is well expressed for his whole life in a curt passage of his "Dialogue." He says of heresy: "There is no fault that more offendeth God." He says of heretics: "Howbeit while they forbare violence, there was little violence done to them."

More was a man so little inconsistent, so little wavering, that his deeds even show his principles, and his philosophy can be read in his actions. If it is asked how More thought heretics should be treated, let the case of Grinaeus be examined. Grinaeus came to England as a Greek scholar bent on editing some corrected texts of Plato and of Proclus. He was a German, a Lutheran. More, by the very same principles with which he had had a boy flogged in his own house, entertained this Lutheran, as a scholar, under his roof and merely saw to it that he did not spread his unfriendly doctrines. After More's death Grinaeus pays his tribute to More's kind of toleration. He dedicated his edition of Proclus to More's son, John, and in that dedication he wrote:

"Your father at that time held the highest rank,

but apart from that, by his own excellent qualities, he was clearly marked out as the chief man of the realm, whilst I was obscure and unknown. Yet for the love of learning in the midst of public and private business he found time to converse much with me: he, the Chancellor of the Kingdom, made me sit at his table: going to and from the Court he took me with him and kept me ever at his side. He had no difficulty in seeing that my religious opinions were on many points different from his own, but his goodness and courtesy were unchanged. Though he differed so much from my views, yet he helped us in word and deed and carried through my business at his own expense. He gave us a young man, of considerable literary attainments, John Harris, to accompany us on our journey, and to the authorities of the University of Oxford he sent a letter couched in such terms that at once not only were the libraries of all the Colleges thrown open to us, but the students, as if they had been touched by the rod of Mercury, showed us the greatest favor. . . . I returned to my country overjoyed at the treasures I had discovered, laden with your father's generous gifts, and almost overwhelmed by his kindness."

More found a way not only to be a loyal Chancellor to a King, of whose policies he did not approve, but also to hold the dignity and lordliness of that Chancellorship without ceasing to be the simple direct Thomas More, known in London. He did not refuse the golden chain for his neck. He maintained now, as was becoming, a grand barge with eight bargemen on the Thames to carry him to and from Westminster. He became an even more hospitable patron of arts and letters, lodged Holbein, the portraitist, in his own house, paid him to depict himself, his father, his family, and introduced him to the King, and launched him on his career of painting a generation of English notables. His house at Chelsea put on in its small way a magnificence reflected from the royal court. Yet all this was done with a smile. In his meditations he mocked at the vanity of worldly magnificence. He showed himself in his intimacy always the same Thomas More that he had always been.

Son-in-law Roper tells two stories of him. As often as on his way through Westminster Hall to his place in the Chancery, he passed that Court of the King's Bench, where his father was judge, he would go into that court, kneel down before his father, and ask his blessing. And the other story tells of how the Duke of Norfolk coming importantly to Chelsea found Lord Chancellor More singing with a surplice on in the parish choir.

"God's body, God's body, my Lord Chancellor," said the Duke. "What! A parish clerk! A parish clerk!"

"Nay," quoth Sir Thomas More, smiling on the

Duke. "Your Grace may not think that the King, your master and mine, will with me for serving God his Master be offended, or thereby account his office dishonored."

But the shadow of the King's wilfulness was all the time drawing nearer and nearer. More could feel it approaching, as you feel the night approaching, when you are busy at work, and have turned your back on that night. Henry had once thought that his successful Chancellor Wolsey could for him threaten the Pope, and secure his divorce, but as soon as Wolsey failed, he decided to do the threatening himself, forgetting that the dangerous thing about making threats is that if he whom you threaten does not give in, then you must put your threat into execution, or be humbled. Henry would do anything rather than be humbled. He first tried to threaten the Pope by an action which looked respectable. He appealed to the Universities to decide whether or not he was truly married. He pretended that the Universities were impartial, whereas the Pope was controlled by the Emperor. And also it gave a chance to the Pope to throw the responsibility on their learned faculties, and to proclaim himself in the face of the Emperor persuaded by them. A man named Cranmer, later to be Archbishop of Canterbury, suggested this move. It was canny but not well carried out. And even though Lord Chancellor More was forced to read its results to Parliament, Parliament was singularly unimpressed, and by it the Pope was not one whit moved.

The next threatenings were more brutal, more direct. If the Pope refused to accede to his desires — which were derived from a wise and Christian conscience — he would rob the Church, which he had hitherto protected, of its wealth and of its liberties. To accomplish the first purpose, the wealth-robbing, he had the hand of the Commons ready to do the work for him. To aid him in his second purpose, the enslavement of the Church, he had the slavishness of the English bishops, who almost without exception were ready, when pursued by the Commons, to run subservient to him for protection.

Parliament met in November 1529. Its work was to be such as to earn for it the murderous name of the "Black Parliament," and there is good reason to suppose that its membership was picked directly by the King in order that it might be willing to serve his evil purpose. As evidence that it was a King-picked Parliament we have More's own reference to it after his condemnation, when he called it a Parliament "ye know how chosen." But wicked or not wicked, Henry taught it first to appear mild, to do no more than show its teeth. Certain bills were proposed in the Commons, which were comparatively harmless, and which were really harmful

only in the sense that they were an interference by
the Temporalty in the Spiritualty, and also in the
vindictive discussion which they provoked. Fisher,
Bishop of Rochester, said that Commons were
acting like heretics. This was taken by the Commons as an unwarranted insult. They complained
to the King. But Fisher was reading their heart,
not their actions. All they did was this. They fined
non-resident bishops, prohibited Churchmen from
holding several benefices (a reform which the Pope
would have been glad to have the power to bring
about himself), and forbade the clergy to own
tanneries and breweries. The Lords at first balked
at these bills. But the King negotiated. They gave
in. At this the King muzzled Parliament. He
thought that the Pope should be given another
chance to grant the divorce. Parliament had shown
its teeth.

But the Pope continued unmoved, and the King
resolved to proceed more drastically. Wolsey in
October, 1529, had been accused of overstepping an
old law of the year 1353 which had tried to limit
the Pope's power of intervention in England
against the will of the King. Everything that
Wolsey had done as Papal Legate had been done
at the King's command, so the charge was a lie
which fooled nobody, but it got rid of Wolsey, and
it led to putting the Church in England into a
curious situation. Wolsey to secure pardon had

pleaded guilty. That meant, so it was said, that the whole nation had been guilty with Wolsey. But the King very royally, very graciously, pardoned the whole nation. He did not pardon the clergy, however, and in January 1531, the clergy was reminded that it was still guilty. Thereupon the Archbishop of Canterbury summoned his spiritual parliament, a Convocation. It met at Westminster, January 21st, and set to work to buy pardon of the King.

If they could not buy that pardon, their goods could legally by the law of 1353, the law of praemunire, be confiscated, and their lives forfeit. They offered £40,000. Not enough, said the King. They offered £100,000. Not enough, said the King. They must, in order to be pardoned, declare that the King was sole protector and supreme head of the Church in England.

The bishops of England were singularly blind to what this proposal involved. They were either blind or cowardly; call them blind. And their blindness was not due to moral depravity. Their lives were more exemplary than those of the bishops in most of the countries of Europe. But they were generally not theologians, but canon lawyers, and as canon lawyers they had often been in the King's employ. They were used to looking to the King. Some of them — five of them in fact — were directly grateful to the King for having recently elevated them to bishoprics. Two were blind by

being over ninety years of age. Four were blind,
being dead, their sees vacant. One was blind; being
a Spaniard, Confessor to the Queen, not understanding English. At any rate the Convocation of
Canterbury was not duly alarmed over the proposal. It squirmed, but showed itself ready to submit.

Only one bishop really showed his mettle, and he
was significantly a theologian, who looked at the
theological connections, rather than the purely
administrative complications, of the proposal. He
was the vigilant exception, John Fisher, of Rochester, who proclaimed that buying pardon at such a
price would lead to schism and heresy. As an individual he had already likened the King to that
Herod whom John the Baptist had rebuked. He
had already told the Commons when in the preceding December they had begun their raid on the
Church's wealth, that they were losing their faith.
He was far-sighted, courageous, but all that he
alone against the frightened others could do was to
have the Convocation add to their acknowledg-
ment of the supremacy of the King, a restriction:
"insofar as the law of Christ allows." So the Convocation was pardoned. And within a month, the
Convocation of York was also pardoned, — that
latter without having added any restriction whatsoever.

More wanted to resign. Like Fisher he saw that

such a move would lead to the debasing of the Spiritualty. The Spiritualty was already losing that effulgence which had once drawn all men's eyes towards it, as an earthly image of paradise. The Spiritualty would lose its prestige. The religiously thirsty would seek consolation in heresy, in a forbidden spring, now that the true spring had lost its appearance of being what it was. To go further with the King might lead him to do things which his conscience could not let him do. Yet More was never precipitate. He would wait till he had an opportunity to resign.

On the thirteenth day of July, 1530, Henry had quitted his wife Catherine for good and all. Henceforth he did not even treat her as queen. A year and a half later he began to treat Anne, if not as a wife, as a queen. "Wherefore the Common people daily murmured and spake their foolish fantasies. But the affairs of Princes be not ordered by the common people, nor it were not convenient that all things were opened to them. — " so wrote Chronicler Hall, a partisan of Henry's. By the beginning of 1532, Anne, herself, was beginning to feel certain of her position. Even if the Pope refused the divorce, she would see to it that it was got from the English clergy, as if they were a separate Church.

In January 1532, a new blow was struck. It was still against the Pope. Parliament was asked to abolish the payment of Annates to Rome —

Annates being the year's revenue paid to the Pope
by every newly-appointed bishop. — Curiously
enough the Commons were not anxious to pass
this. They were more for robbing the clergy, than
for attacking Rome. Suppression of the annates
would not enrich them. But Henry entered their
chamber, was present at their vote, asking them
to vote visibly by moving to this or that side of the
hall. Annates were suppressed.

At the same time, at the King's instigation, the
Commons presented to the King "a supplication
against the Ordinaries," asking that the Convocation of the Clergy be deprived of their right to
legislate on spiritual matters independent of the
King, and of Parliament. The hearts of the Commoners were not wholly in their request, for it was
not their affair, not a money affair; and they asked
to be prorogued after its presentation and to be
allowed to proceed back to their homes. Their
business needed to be taken care of.

But Henry kept them to their task. They were
asked to hand on this bill for the "submission of
the clergy," from the King to the Convocation of
the Clergy, and to wait an answer. The Convocation after a feeble struggle at compromise, agreed
to give up its rights to make canon laws without
royal consent. And, besides that, it consented that
a committee, half of it made up of laymen, should
revise the church laws. Thomas More, even though

Chancellor, opposed this supplication against the Ordinaries, he opposed the exaction of the consequent submission from the clergy. While the Convocation was giving in, he took advantage of a real excuse; a malady in his chest, to resign from the Chancellorship.

Chapter X

MORE'S RETIREMENT

More now wrote his own epitaph. This was not an act of self-pity. It was an act of bravado. As such he recognized it. His letter to Erasmus describes the wording of the epitaph as not false, but possibly boastful. He wrote that epitaph partly for himself as a reminder of death, partly for the world in his own justification. In definite letters cut in marble he presented the record of his stewardship. There were calumnies abroad that he had been cast out of office by the King. Tyndale really believed, and Germany was being led to believe, that the King had ousted him for his too great severity to heretics. More wished to state the truth, stoutly, incisively.

He recounted his ancestry. He was of honest if not noble parentage. He paid his tribute to three people: the King, Cuthbert Tunstall, and his father. The first had earned the right to hold, first among kings, the title "Defender of the Faith." He had honored More, raising him from office to office until he was Lord Chancellor of England. Cuthbert Tunstall, his friend, and fellow ambassa-

dor, was so wise and virtuous, the world scarcely
had in wisdom and virtue his equal. His father,
John More, had lived to see his son Thomas More
Lord Chancellor, and then had died. He was a man
"civil, pleasant, hurtful to no man, just and un-
corrupted." Then he boasted for himself. He, as
the King's ambassador had by the Treaty of
Cambrai brought to pass a long-looked-for peace,
"which peace Our Lord stablish and make perpetual." In all public office he had earned the
approval of his prince. He had been not odious to
the nobles, nor unpleasant to the people. Then his
Latin — for the epitaph was in Latin — stated
boldly that he had been gracious to all; bothersome
only to thieves, murderers and heretics: ("furibus
autem, et homicidis, haereticisque molestus.")

The rest of the epitaph concerned the future:
death. He had resigned the Chancellorship because
of a malady in his breast. His virtuous King had
accepted that resignation. He had transported his
first wife — uxorcula Mori — to be buried beneath
the same epitaph where he was to be buried. In
order that he should not fear death, and in order
that after death he should find the tomb "a gate to
a wealthier life," he asked the prayers of every
reader of that epitaph.

The writer of the epitaph could order a marble
slab for his own tomb, but he was no longer a rich
man. He had married off his children to wives and

husbands decently propertied. Otherwise he had
shown no worldly prudence. He had spent what he
gained yearly in enriching the poor, and in maintaining that dignity which high office forced upon
him. He had also supported that little commonwealth of his family, all under his roof, four wives,
four husbands, besides himself and his wife, and
his father, while he lived, and his father's third
wife, and eleven grandchildren, and some guests
like Holbein, and other poorer guests, and other
relatives, and numerous necessary servants, and
sometimes a heretic whom he was treating kindly.
And now there was no longer the King's pay, nor
any income from the law, nor any King's pension.
All that was left to More was less than a hundred
pounds a year. And he had his great house on his
hands. He was forced to throw ferns into the fire-
places to give his house a touch of warmth. He
could not afford fire-wood.

More showed no panic at this new prospect. He
dismissed his servants, but not until he had found
places for them. He placed his eight barge-men
with Lord Audley his profiteering successor in the
Chancellorship. Henceforward they could row
about a man who had lost that part of human nature called integrity, and who was so safely free
from religious sensibilities that he was willing to be
the sole bidder for St. Botolph's Church, Aldgate,
later to be confiscated by the King, in order that

he might turn it into a stone quarry. As for disbanding his family, More was opposed to it. He would prefer that they continue to live together sharing expenses. He had lived, he said, during his life on three very spare diets: Lincoln's Inn fare, New Inn fare, Oxford fare. He listed them in order of their spareness — Oxford being the most spare. He and his children would first try to maintain the Lincoln's Inn standard. If that was impossible, they would change, and see if Oxford fare — which kept alive "Many grave, learned, fathers" — might not keep them alive. After that they could all go abegging together, singing Salve Regina at every man's door, and thus keeping merry.

They did not all go abegging together. The household broke up. He was left alone with his wife, and at least two faithful servants: a girl called Dorothy Colley, a man called John a Wood. But even though only a much diminished household remained, it was not a downcast household. Nor was it an idle one. The doctors declared that More might yet mend from his malady. His illness was not mortal, and it could not keep him from one labor which was not yet through: the defence of the Spiritualty. He was still in controversy with Tyndale, finishing his "Confutation," going on to his "Apology."

But More was not to be allowed to remain undisturbed in his retirement. In the first place there

was spite to attack him. The party of Anne Boleyn
knew that he was, both at heart and in secret words
to the King, opposed to Henry's repudiation of
Catherine. They saw that, even though the excuse
of a malady was a true one, his resignation was a
rebuke to them. They wished to punish Thomas
More therefore and also, for their future, to dis-
credit him. What they did was not adroit. Certainly it was not successful. They brought various
charges against him to prove he had been a corrupt
Chancellor.

How More freed himself from the charges can be
well illustrated by one story. The story shows that
"young More," as he had till last year been called,
was not, though retired and exhausted, anything
but still young in spirit. He was also still the im-
provisor of comedies. Listen to the comedy, which
took place before the Privy Council. A man named
Parnell, accused More of having taken a gold cup
from a Mrs. Vaughan, who was the wife of a Mr.
Vaughan in whose favor More had decided a suit
against this accuser, Parnell. More acknowledged
that such a gift had been made, — yes, a New
Year's gift, — some time after the decision.

Then exclaimed that clumsy father of Anne
Boleyn's, that man without a forehead, now Earl
of Wiltshire: "Ah! did I not tell you, my lords, that
you would find the matter true!"

A due dramatic pause! — Then More at perfect

and mischievous leisure went on. Yes, he had
received that gift, he had sent his butler scurrying
off to fetch wine to fill it. He had pledged Mrs.
Vaughan's health. She had pledged his. Then he had
given her back the cup as a present to her husband.

Had it been only for Anne Boleyn's party, and
for the King's own feelings, More might have remained in retirement, writing against Barnes,
Saint-German, Tyndale, Frith; for the spite of the
Earl of Wiltshire was a bit blundering, and the
King's feelings always inclined naturally to gen-
erosity when no stronger emotion assailed him.
For instance the King had commanded Lord
Audley and the Duke of Norfolk, both of them, to
pronounce panegyrics on More at More's retirement, and he himself had declared himself as quite
free from resentment. But there was another man
on the scene, not a sentimentalist, not a bungler: a
man, like Wolsey, lowly-born, but not like Wolsey
devoid of imagination. He was more cold-blooded
than Wolsey, certainly more keen-sighted. Personal ambition he evidently possessed, but he was
also actuated by that less personal thing, the desire
of an inventor to see what he has invented work.
It had never occurred to the able but imaginative
Wolsey that by his success or his failures he could
change the system of government in England —
that is, the fundamental system based on the relation of the Spiritualty to the Temporalty.

This man on the other hand deliberately planned
to unite the Spiritualty and the Temporalty under
one authority, which happened to be the Temporalty. In other words he would try to bring about
the state of affairs in defence of which Saint-German was arguing in his theorizing solitude. The
result of the new system would be a much greater
national efficiency. Collisions between the Temporalty and the Spiritualty would be avoided. A
smooth-running autonomous state would arise,
which could make not only its own human laws, but
its own laws of God. It could if not conquer at
least defy the universe. What if the Church was en-
slaved by the State? The Church would make a
good slave. What if the enslavement of the Church,
brought about its abasement, and then the consequent decay of religion, and then the consequent
decay of the State itself? Well, that was a consequence too remote to be thought about. So moved
the mind of this man who was both a man of action
and of imagination, an inventor of a machine of
government. His name was Thomas Cromwell.

Cromwell was, in office, merely Secretary to the
King, but he was in an excellent position to have
his invention adopted. He could treat other people
as puppets, notably the King. The King cared not
particularly for Cromwell's invention; but he did
care to have Anne Boleyn his wife and England's
Queen. In order to gain Anne Boleyn he was willing

to make himself what Cromwell was so anxious for him to become: supreme head both of the Temporalty and the Spiritualty.

Cromwell played well with the King, and also he seemed to win fortune to his side. There was one particular difficulty in the way of making Henry master of the Church. Warham, the Archbishop of Canterbury, was an old man, sorry for having compromised as he had. He was in a position to, and ready to, withstand the King. But on the August that followed More's retirement he died, as if at Cromwell's command. There was a new Archbishop ready at hand: Cranmer, a timid man, an eloquent man, at that moment ambassador of the King's to Germany to the Court of Charles V. That he was married secretly in Germany made no difference. Let him come back. And he did come back, hiding his wife for the channel-crossing in a barrel, and reminding us thereby that More may have been right when he accused the priests, turned Lutheran, and so prone thereon to marry, of having not the respect for marriage that they pretended. He noticed with amazement and amusement the punishment suggested by Tyndale for friars: that they be whipped naked through the streets and then be made to marry — keeping, I suppose, the worst punishment for the last.

Cranmer would be created Archbishop of Canterbury after the old fashion. That is the King would send his name to the Pope. The Pope would approve the choice, and send him his pallium. But then — and this was in Cromwell's and Anne Boleyn's mind, — Cranmer, who was secretly more heretic even than Henry suspected, would lead his flock away from the Pope, and win Henry's favor in so doing by granting the King his divorce, and by helping him handily to Anne Boleyn. All was running so smoothly that even before Cranmer had returned from Germany Henry was on the Continent travelling with Anne Boleyn. Probably Cromwell had promised her she should now be queen. He may have wondered if it were not better to delay the marriage until it was certain she could bear Henry a child. By January 1533, she was with child, and was then secretly married, — if you care to call it married. Everything was going very smoothly: both Cromwell and the King could be satisfied.

As soon as Cranmer had in the Spring been elevated by the Pope to his destined see, things marched even more quickly. The puppets were all in place. Cranmer acted with well-planned indignation, summoned the King to appear before him for having lived in adultery with Catherine of Aragon during twenty years. — The King confessed his guilt, repudiated Catherine, and received pardon from a lordly Archbishop. The marriage of Henry and Catherine was then by Cranmer annulled. Forthwith there passed through the streets of London a procession, in it a white-faced lady sitting by a king. She was sick, but she had succeeded. She was going to be crowned. She was crowned. And the populace watched the procession, sullen. The men kept their hats on their heads. They did not bother about things in the abstract, and therefore seemed unduly pliant and subservient. But they showed themselves, stubborn and manful, when they really understood what was going on.

There was one man not in the crowd, not even in it with his hat on, that man Thomas More. The King had indirectly asked him to be present. Dignitaries friendly to More — Bishop Tunstall, for example — were persuaded to urge More to attend the Coronation. He was offered, ever so kindly, a new velvet suit. More refused the invitation and the offer. He explained his refusal by a story. There was an Emperor once who had decreed severe death-penalties against certain offenders, but who had out of esteem for virginity, exempted virgins from such punishments even if they offended. What was the Emperor's quandary! The first offender proved to be a virgin. What could be done? A wise man suggested that the virgin first be deflowered so that then she could be legally devoured. More's comment was that he could not keep himself from being devoured, but he was not going to be deflowered first.

More's absence from the coronation irritated the King and Anne Boleyn. It found Thomas Cromwell less sensitive. He wanted More's approval not of the new marriage, but of the new system of government which he hoped to initiate. Moreover he felt sure that he could secure More's approval of it, either by promise or by threat for with all his canniness he was blind to the higher motives of men. In the fall of 1533, after Anne Boleyn had given to the world the future Queen Elizabeth, the King's Privy Council, with which More had been associated for twelve years, published nine articles of which the two most important said that "causes" should not be removed from the country where they were initiated — hence no appeals to the Pope, — and that a General Council is superior to all bishops, and of which the least important, — because most puerile, — announced that the Pope was by birth illegitimate, and guilty first of simony, and then, by refusing the King's appeal, of heresy. These articles made reconciliation with the Pope almost impossible; they would serve also to make a man like More declare his mind. More said nothing except in his heart, but a pamphlet appeared remonstrating at those nine articles, a pamphlet which Cromwell pretended to think emanated from More. More wrote a letter to Cromwell explaining that he had written no such pamphlet, that he did not consider himself learned enough, or enough instructed in the facts to pass judgment on those articles.

There came another chance to catch More. The chance arose owing to the sayings of a certain Benedictine nun: Elizabeth Barton, sometimes called the Nun of Canterbury, sometimes the Holy Maid of Kent. This nun had not in her first womanhood planned to be a nun. She had been a serving-maid subject to epilepsy, who had been cured of her affliction in a chapel of Our Lady. Thereupon she became a Benedictine, and attracted attention not only by her cure, and by her profession, but by certain private revelations, which she experienced, and which by some were regarded as divinely inspired. She had finally gained great notoriety, and even fame, by openly attacking the project of the King's remarriage, and by threatening him with divine punishment.

It is almost impossible not to feel on the side of this Maid of Kent, not because anybody knows enough to be sure that her revelations were genuine, but simply because she was the one person in England except for England's John the Baptist, Bishop Fisher, who had the courage to say what so many felt. Also it is quite certain that she was unjustly treated. Her revelations were distorted. Her illiteracy was played with, as that of St. Joan of Arc less successfully was played with. She was made to seem to have made a complete confession

of her guilt as a fraud and a traitor in St. Paul's
churchyard, and then finally six months later was
executed with some priests, — so-called accomplices. She may have been half-mad, or self-
deluded, but she was certainly not a scheming con-
spirator. And she was not executed for her own
wickedness, for she had none, and Cromwell knew
she had none, but in order to give an impression
that there was conspiracy abroad. It was hoped
that through her downfall might be inculpated
various prominent men, who were known to have
known her; — among them Bishop Fisher and
Thomas More.

Cromwell blessed the affair of the Maid of Kent.
Both More and Fisher had had conversations with
the nun. They could be classed as traitors. They
could be threatened with death. If they were
brought ordinarily to trial, they might and would
prove their innocence, and possibly that of the nun.
Fortunately, however, Cromwell had found a trick
to avoid such trials. Taking advantage of a device
called attainder, which had a legitimate place in
the English laws, whereby Parliament could punish
a traitor by depriving him of his life, and his blood
of their rights as citizens, — he did not have to
resort to the law courts. Parliament could commit
murder for him. More's name and Fisher's name
were included in the Bill of Attainder which was to
put the nun to death, as if she and as if they had

been interested in politics, fomenting rebellion. It was Cromwell, Cromwell's own handwriting that inserted the names, — not the King's. He would extort submission from two men who though brave, were human and would give in. Their submission for the well-working of his invention was necessary.

More did not give in. Fisher did not give in. More knew who was plotting against him, and he chose Cromwell, — and sometimes the King — to whom to write. He wrote to Cromwell at great length. He acknowledged that he had met the nun at least nine years ago, but then only at the suggestion of the King, who wished to know what More thought of her. Later on during the last few years he had talked with her again and had found her in appearance humble. She had seemed to him holy, and her holiness was all that he had been interested in. He had forbidden her to talk with him about the King's affairs, or the marriage. He had even written her a letter (which very likely Cromwell possessed) in which he warned her to keep herself out of things not her province: "It sufficeth me, Good madam, to put you in remembrance of such things as I nothing doubt your wisdom and the Spirit of God shall keep you from talking with any person, specially with high persons, of any such manner things as pertain to prince's affairs, or the state of the realm, but only to commune and talk with any person, high and low, of any such manner things as may to the soul be profitable for you to show, and for them to know."

Letters to Cromwell and to the King did not prevent More's name and Fisher's name from staying in the Bill. Then More asked what was his right: a hearing before the House of Lords. This was disconcerting, for the Lords admired More, and More was wonderfully eloquent. Once they listened to him they would undoubtedly refuse to punish him the terrible traitor's punishment, and in order to throw out his name would have to throw out the whole bill. Cromwell, therefore, named a special committee: Audley; the Duke of Norfolk; Archbishop Cranmer; and Cromwell; to listen to More in place of the Lords.

This committee had no belief that for the affair of the Maid it could convict More, but it had a singular belief that by bribes and threats it could arrive at a better success. It told him how much the King loved him, how kind the King had been to him, how ready the King was to give him anything he asked, if he would express his approval of the King's marriage policy. He thanked them, thanked the King, refused.

Then threats began and false charges. More, it was said, had been a crafty traitor to his King luring him in that book of his, in defense of the Seven Sacraments, to overstate the powers and eminence of the Pope. More contradicted them flatly, saying that he on the contrary had tried to soften the King's manner of describing the Papal authority, and that the King had held to it, and that the King himself knew that this was true. As for the vague threats which were given to him "My lords" quoth he, "these terrors be arguments for children, and not for me." The Duke of Norfolk reminded him that it is perilous to strive with princes: "Indignatio principis mors est." "Is that all, my lord?" quoth he. "Then in good faith the difference between your grace and me is but this, that I shall die today, and you tomorrow."

More was very merry that night when he returned home. His son-in-law Roper thought it must be that the Bill of Attainder had been dropped. Not at all, explained More. He had forgotten all about the Bill. "Wilt thou know, son Roper, why I was so merry? In good faith I rejoiced that I had given the devil a foul fall, and that with those lords I had gone so far as, without no shame, I could never go back again."

Up to this point More had retreated like a wary commander. He had not even defended the Nun of Canterbury as our enthusiasm often wishes he had. He did not, for instance, cry out that her confession was false. He was too much a lawyer to do such a thing. No one had appointed him judge of the matter. He was in no position to prove such a remonstrance. He had simply said what as a private citizen he could say of her from his own private observation. He had been calm and calculating in every move. Now he calculated that he could retreat no further.

Cromwell saw that More had taken up his stand, but he dared not attack him. He let the Privy Council go down on their knees and persuade the King — whose wilfulness now wanted to keep More's name in the Bill — to erase More's name — More's name and Fisher's. He assured the King and Anne Boleyn that very soon he would have a better trap in which to catch these old-fashioned obstinate men. More knew what the new trap would be: the device of the oaths. He wrote a letter, meanwhile, to Cromwell, so that there should be no misunderstanding as to his position. As for the Maid of Kent, he had said what he had to say in regard to her. The King knew what he thought about the annulment. It was the King's affair, and nobody else's; the views that he had expressed on the matter. They were private views.

In regard to the question of the Pope's Supremacy he was more bold, for that affair was his affair insofar as it concerned his conscience, and the ultimate salvation of his soul. He had, he said, spent ten years studying the Doctors of the Church from the early Saint Ignatius who was disciple to Saint John the Evangelist, down to his own day and he could find no worthy opinion which could make him think that he could deny the divine institution of the Supremacy of the Pope over the universal church and not by that denial endanger his soul. He believed that the Supremacy of the Pope was necessary and convenient, but, above and beyond that, lay the fact which affected his conscience: the Supremacy of the Pope had been divinely instituted.

Yet where his conscience was not concerned he was willing to be compliant to the King's will. He would not meddle with those who thought differently than he did about the affair of Supremacy. That his word in such a promise could be trusted was attested to by his past conduct. He had, it is true, some ten years ago raised the Pope to high eminence in a Latin work of his, but that was at the King's behest, and for the King's defense. Since that he had written many English pages of religious controversy, but never in that controversy had he dwelt on the position of the Papacy in any way that could offend the King, — even now in the King's present mind, — and once he had crossed out some lines already written for the reason that they might be twisted to seem to be against the King. He had been obedient, and would be obedient where obedience was due.

The King had claimed that Pope Clement VII was not really the Pope because he had bought his election, and was therefore, a simonist, and following that line of attack, had appealed to a General Council to unseat the Pope. More did not claim that the King had no right to appeal to such a Council. He did not judge the affair himself and say indignantly that the Pope was not a simonist. He took a lawyer's attitude: Let the King appeal to the General Council. It may declare the Pope's election invalid. Then a new Pope more friendly to Henry may be elected.

While More was writing this letter, the Easter of 1534 was drawing near. It was a date for special reasons that year dramatic, for Henry VIII had made it the date on which his ultimatum to the Pope expired: if the Pope did not recognize the annulment of his marriage to Catherine before Easter, then he would cease to dally with the Pope. He would cut off England from its allegiance to the Pope. On the preceding June the Pope had already pronounced a decision favorable to Catherine. It was almost impossible that he could reverse it. But Francis I, King of France, bent in his wiser instincts on keeping Christendom united, prayed Henry to wait until the consistory of Cardinals met. Pretext might yet be found to favor Anne Boleyn. On the twenty-third of March 1534, the Cardinals voted nineteen to three that the first marriage of Henry was valid. Anne's marriage with Henry was not a marriage at all.

Parliament was ready to act. Once upon a time Parliament had been frightened of the Pope. Leaving out spiritual fear, it had had a temporal fear of him. When the Pope excommunicated a king, or placed a kingdom under an interdict, it had hurt trade. English merchants had feared until recently that the Pope could destroy English commerce with Flanders, by turning the Emperor, sovereign of Flanders, into a crusader against England. But suddenly the English merchants, and Parliament had had their eyes opened. Trade had become so important that it could not be interfered with for religious reasons. Neither on the continent nor in England was policy being dictated by spiritual motives. Parliament was ready to act. It acted.

On Monday in Holy Week, March 30th, an Act of Succession was passed. It deprived Mary, daughter of Catherine, of her right to succeed her father, and established Anne Boleyn's issue as the first in succession. Anyone who opposed the new succession was guilty of high treason, and, in order to make sure that it should be carried out, an oath to defend and maintain that act was demanded of every lord spiritual or temporal in the land, and of every subject who had come of age, according as the King or his inheritors might designate. The precise formula of the oath was not specified. Hence Cromwell and the Privy Council could word that oath as they saw fit. They could attach pre-

ambles to it. They did attach preambles to it: this
for a spiritual lord, that for a temporal lord. In both
cases they were able by that preamble to turn the
oath into an oath acknowledging the spiritual
supremacy of the King.

The Commons swore the oath: among their
members, William Roper, son-in-law to Thomas
More. The Lords swore the oath. The bishops
swore the oath, all except Fisher who had been
detained in prison ever since he had been accused
of complicity with Elizabeth Barton. Now of those
subjects, who were of age, and who could be asked
by the King to swear that oath, there stood foremost and inevitably Thomas More. He knew that
he would be called on, accustomed himself to the
thought of so being summoned, prepared his
family as well as possible for what might else have
come to them as a blow, and waited.

Good Friday passed. Easter passed. No sum-
mons. On Low Sunday he went to London with
son-in-law Roper to hear a sermon there at St.
Paul's Cross. After that sermon an official followed
him, and overtook him as he entered the house of
his adopted daughter Margaret Giggs who had
married his Grecian friend John Clements. More
was to appear the next morning at Lambeth before
the Royal Commissioners to take like everybody
else the oath.

The next day was April 13th. He began the day

by receiving Holy Communion. It was his custom
on the great days of his life. This was a great day.
He said good-bye to his family, but would not allow
them to follow him nearer to the river than the
wicket-gate. — "Deliver us from temptation." —
He shut the gate after him, got into Roper's boat,
and appeared down-cast as he was rowed down-
river. Suddenly he turned to Roper, brightened:
"Son Roper, I thank Our Lord the field is won."

And now the grave commissioners were seated at
Lambeth waiting for him. They were the same
commission as at the previous hearing, except that
the Abbot of Westminster had replaced the Duke
of Norfolk. There was a file of other men waiting
there also to be offered the oath. More, however,
was the only layman. They called on him, the only
layman, to take the oath first. Let him give the
good example. "Then desired I the sight of the Act
of Succession," says More, "which was delivered
me in a printed roll. After which read secretly by
myself, and the oath considered with the Act, I
answered unto them that my purpose was not to
put any fault either in the Act or any man that
made it, or in the oath or any man that sware it,
nor to condemn the conscience of any other man:
but as for myself, in good faith my conscience so
moved me in the matter, that though I would not
deny to swear to the succession, yet unto that oath
that there was offered me I could not swear without

the jeoparding of my soul to perpetual damna-
tion." In other words More refused to take the
oath because attached to it was a preamble assert-
ing the supremacy of the King over the Spiritualty.
It was not for More, private citizen, to decide who
should succeed Henry VIII on England's throne.
It was very much his affair, as a Christian, not to
take an oath contrary to his religion.

At More's refusal the commissioners expressed
suavely their sorrow and regretted to have to avow
the King's Highness might take his refusal amiss.
And they showed him a long list of names of those
who had already signed the oath. In what good
society of names he would be if he also signed!

They sent More downstairs to wait in the garden. It was too hot in the garden, says More, on this
April day so he waited in an old burned chamber
that looked on the garden. In that garden he saw
what he, who had seen many pageants, called a
pageant. It was played for his benefit. He saw one
man, formerly a chaplain of the King, Dr. Wilson
go off to the Tower. He also had refused the oath.
Bishop Fisher who had been brought before the
commissioners, and had of course, as his previous
conduct foretold, refused the oath, was not paraded
through the garden. It might have been heartening
so to see him. He was kept for the moment indoors.
Then those who had taken the oath were led by,
and O how happy they were shown! It was a hot

day and the Vicar of Croydon, called out in dryness and gladness for drink from the buttery bar. Such conviviality among those who had signed!

"When they had played their pageant and were gone out of the place, then I was called in again." — So says More. The commissioners asked him to disclose why he refused to take the oath. He answered frankly that he feared the King would be displeased at him for refusing the oath. He did not wish further to exasperate His Highness by giving his reasons.

At this they called him stubborn, which he did not want to be, so he consented to give his reasons provided he should have the King's word that the reasons he gave would not be used to incriminate him. This privilege was refused him. How then, he asked, could they call it obstinacy on his part to try to keep himself out of peril?

After this homely bit of wisdom, the Archbishop of Canterbury had his say. He was not maladroit. He argued that since More was in doubt about the oath, but perfectly sure that he should be loyal to the King, was it not wise therefore that he should do what he was sure of, and forget what he was doubtful about? Just how to answer this, More, by his own confession, was perplexed. He acknowledged that it was so sudden and subtle an argument, that all he could say was that this was one of the cases where his conscience could not obey his prince. And then came a flash of his repartee. Did this mean, he asked, if wherever there was a theological dispute, the King's commandment would solve all doubts?

Then the Abbot of Westminster had his say. He did not argue, not this counterfeit son of Saint Benedict. He, with Pax still as his motto, and false Pax in his heart, preached the noble thing humility. Was not More afraid to set his own mind: one against so many? More insisted that he was not setting himself up alone. He was conforming, if not to the Council of the realm, to the general council of Christendom. Then he looked at his judges. And his look made them feel that they rather than he were singular.

Lord Audley was too much a dullard to speak, but Thomas Cromwell took his turn. He played neither the theologian, nor the preacher. He played the friend. He exclaimed that he would rather have his only son lose his head rather than have Thomas More refuse this oath. It would make the King think More had been an accomplice to the Nun of Canterbury. More replied that the opposite was known to be true, and even though his move might be misunderstood, yet he could not take the oath.

Cromwell went on: Would not More take the oath of succession without the preamble which related to the Papal supremacy? Yes, indeed More would, but he must be allowed to phrase that oath.

Then burst in Lord Audley: "Marry, Master Secretary, mark that too, that he will not swear that neither but under some certain manner."

The hearing was over. It was over quickly as if Lord Audley wished it to appear that More had refused every kind of an oath. More was lodged with the Abbot of Westminster. It could not be decided whether he should be sent home or to the Tower. The judges were used to dealing with all sorts of men except those who put the Spiritualty in its proper place. He could not therefore be understood, nor dealt with.

Cranmer's subtlety had an idea. Could not More be led to take the Oath of Succession without the preamble, — he and Fisher? That would smooth things over. News would run abroad of their submission, and it might be suppressed just what kind of oaths they had taken. Cranmer wrote a letter to Cromwell suggesting this piece of straightforwardness.

Cromwell wrote an answer. He said that the King's Grace wished the oaths to be sworn to in their entirety with their preamble. Otherwise the whole King's cause might fall to the ground. Otherwise the people, seeing the example of More and Fisher, might think that More and Fisher were confirming the authority of the Bishop of Rome — which was true.

On April 17th More was sent from the Abbot of Westminster's to the Tower.

Chapter XI

THE TOWER OF LONDON

More was at last a Carthusian. He who had considered himself unworthy of a life in a cell, was by God's and the King's behest sent to the Tower of London, there to live in a cell more penitential than ever was Carthusian's. This thrusting upon him of a way of life which he had regarded and shrunk from as beyond his powers, was for him an honor — like a post of danger to a soldier — a late payment, a reward, a promotion in rank. It was, moreover, on one who liked jests, and whimsical turns, a jest played by God, and with that jest he was hilarious.

Sir Richard Cromwell it was who came to conduct him to the Tower; a man who had married the niece of Master Secretary Cromwell, and who by changing his name to Cromwell had shown himself ready to follow more wholly the cause of that family. True to its ambition he was to be a great devourer of monastic lands, and successful in his aspirations, progenitor of a ruler of England, Oliver Cromwell. He saw, with an eye not unused to remarking gold, the chain of gold around More's neck, which More in spite of his soberness, wore as ex-chancellor. He gave thrifty advice to Sir Thomas More, did Sir Richard, for he advised him to send home that valuable chain to his wife or his children.

"No, Sir," quoth Sir Thomas, "that I will not; for if I were taken to the field by mine enemies, I would they should somewhat fare the better by me."

Landed at the Tower, Master Lieutenant, Sir Edmund Walsingham, met him; and by the Lieutenant stood the Porter, which latter knew the traditions of his great office. The Porter demanded of More his upper garment.

"Master Porter," said More, "here it is," and he took off his cap and delivered it to him, saying: "I am very sorry it is no better for you."

"No, Sir," quoth the Porter, "I must have your gown."

Then More was conducted to his cell in Beauchamp Tower, being there led (as is guest by hotel proprietor), by the same Master Lieutenant. John a Wood, More's servant, followed carrying the baggage, some spare clothes, a few books. More turned to John a Wood and merrily before the Master Lieutenant, made his servitor, who obviously could not read or write, swear that if More wrote anything against the King, he should immediately bring it to the Lieutenant.

As soon as he had settled himself in this new apartment he wrote a letter to his daughter, Meg, telling her just what had happened at Lambeth, and what he had said, and what the commissioners had said. The news was not only for Meg, but for all the world. It was prolix and picturesque. Then by Cromwell's permission Meg was allowed to come to see him. She pitied him. You could see that in her face. She pitied him too much. Wherefore, after More, as was his custom with his daughter on her visits, had recited with her the seven psalms and the litany of the saints, he cheered her up:

"I believe, Meg, that they that have put me here ween that they have done me a high displeasure: but I assure thee on my faith, mine good daughter, if it had not been for my wife and ye that be my children (whom I account the chief part of my charge) I would not have failed long ere this to have closed myself in as strait a room, and straiter too. But since I am come hither without mine own desert, I trust that God of His goodness will discharge me of my care, and with his gracious help supply my lack to you. I find no cause, I thank God, Meg, to reckon myself in worse case here than in mine own house, for me thinketh God maketh me a wanton, and setteth me on his lap, and dandleth me."

It was a harder life, for all of "God's dandling,"

than is that of a Carthusian. A Carthusian has
humble amenities, and great spiritual strengthen-
ings, which More was not to enjoy. He was still
so much in the world as to have to pay for his
board: fifteen shillings a week: ten for himself,
five for his servant. He had to pay for that board
out of money which his wife brought him, but
which at last she could not find to bring him, not
even by selling her gay apparel. That he should
so bring her to penury was a pain to his heart.
And, as to his body, the fare — at the King's
command, who wished to bully More into submission — grew worse and worse. Even the Lieutenant of the Tower grew ashamed of what he
offered More. He apologized, said that for his
part he would be glad to entertain More handsomely.

"Master Lieutenant," answered More, "I verily
believe, as you may, you are my good friend indeed, and would, as you say, with your best
cheer entertain me, for which I must heartily
thank you. And assure yourself, Master Lieutenant, I do not mislike my cheer, but whenso-
ever I so do, then you may thrust me out of doors."

At first he was allowed to walk not far out of
doors, but in the Tower yard, and was allowed
to see his Meg and his wife at decent intervals,
for it was still hoped that he might be softened and
won by kindness. But when that failed, severity

was tried. He was now locked in his cell. He was denied the happiness of seeing familiar faces. As summer changed into winter, he had not even the ferns to throw into a fireplace to warm him. He suffered from the stone and from cramps in his legs, and twice he was so feeble he thought he should die, and was content to die. And all this he had to suffer in a confinement far stricter than that of Carthusians, for they have first their cell, and then their solitary garden for each one of them, and their workshop, and they have, aside from their isolation, their sense of community: their gathering together in the choir; and they have the heavenly consolation of the Mass, and they unite with the whole church in its procession through the liturgical year. More in comparison to them was in his grave. No Mass for him. No sacraments. No gathering in choir. No happy bondage. No companionship visible. One hour like another. One day like another. He lived, none-the-less, with the Church Universal, gaily changing his worn clothes to slightly better clothes on the feast days of the Church. And his beard grew long, and longer, and it turned white, and his body grew emaciated into a skeleton, and his eyes grew brighter and more piercing, and they alone seemed to join him to the living. Yet he was happy and his heart overflowed in these words:

"In prison was Joseph while his brethren were

at large, and yet often were his brethren fain to seek upon him for bread.

"In prison was Daniel, and the wild lions about him: and yet even there God kept him harmless, and brought him safe out again.

"If we think that he will not do the likewise for us, let us not doubt but he will do for us, either the like or better. For better may he do for us if he suffer us there to die.

"Saint John, the Baptist, was (you wot well) in prison, while Herod and Herodias sat full merry at the feast, and the daughter of Herodias delighted them with her dancing, till with her dancing she danced off Saint John's head. And now sitteth he with great feast in heaven at God's board, while Herod and Herodias full heavily sit in hell, burning both twain, and to make then sport withal, the Devil with the damsel dance in the fire afore them.

"Finally, cousin, to finish this piece with, Our Saviour was himself take prisoner for our sake, and prisoner was he carried, and prisoner was he kept, and prisoner was he brought forth before Annas, and prisoner was he carried from Caiaphas unto Pilate, and prisoner was he sent from Pilate to King Herod, prisoner from Herod to Pilate again, and so kept as prisoner to the end of his passion."

These lines More wrote in a written meditation,

for like a man born with a pen in his hand, he
meditated best when that hand was not penless.
Besides prayers, letters, verses, he wrote in the
Tower, in its dampness, and silence, treatises on
the Passion of Our Lord, and on the Blessed Sacrament, but he wrote most important of all "A
Dialogue of Comfort Against Tribulation." I say
most important of all not because it is necessarily
most profound, but because it is the most repre-
sentative of all More's works. It is his Divine
Comedy. It talks in terms of all his experience,
puts all his problems in place. It was from this
dialogue that I quoted the lines about imprisonment, and in that dialogue can be found that
More, the poet, who might have become a humanistic idler. And More the Logical thinker is
there, defining the causes of tribulation, and the
kinds of tribulation there are. And More the
jester is there, and More the playwright, feigning a dialogue between two men, an old Anthony,
a young Vincent, two Hungarians who discuss
the prospects before them when they foresee that
their country is to be overrun by the Turks. More
the friend of Erasmus is there, mischief-making
in the very sub-title of the piece: "Made By An
Hungarian in Laten, and translated oute of Laten
into Frenche, and oute of Frenche into Englishe,"
and still friend to Erasmus in traditional satire
against that talkative woman or this hypocrite.

The dialogue was written in prison, in adversity, but it is a continuation or a remodelling of a "Treatise on the Four Last Things" which More had half-written ten years before, less cheerfully in full prosperity. It resumes the threads of many others of his discourses, spoken and written, Latin and English. There is only one More absent from it; More the controversialist. Several times he mentions heretics but it is only to leave them as soon as possible: "Strive will I not with them" he says "for this matter now." Deeper than the More who disputed was the More who prayed, praying that he might meet his enemies turned friends in heaven. This praying More is everywhere present in this "Dialogue of Comfort Against Tribulation."

More wrote this dialogue not really for his friends, not for us who need it and reprint it, but for himself. It was his reckoning. He had that medieval passion of putting thoughts in order. So many questions there were that came to his not-spoiled mind, and so many true and so many false answers. It is not a book of blind bravado; optimism of a kind till recently prescribed for all difficulties, "that things will get better and better." It is skeptic, penetrating, piercing through appearances, to what is lasting and just. "How can a man resist temptation?" he asks. "The manner of the fight against his temptation," says More, "must stand in three things, that is to wit, in resisting, and in contemning, and in the invocation of help.

"Resist must a man for his own part with reason, considering what a folly it were to fall where he need not, while he is not driven to it in avoiding of any other pain or in hope of winning any manner of pleasure, but contrary wise should by that pain, lose everlasting bliss, and fall into everlasting pain."

More's prayers in the Tower during a year must have been long, and profound, and intimate, and well-heard, — if we may judge by the stout strength of spirit he gained from God in spite of in a body racked and distraught. So much for the invocation of help.

Contemning (which meant laughing at the Devil) he had also practised, for he was not untrained in mockery. The Devil, says More, being a proud spirit "cannot endure to be mocked."

Reason is also all important, for men are not animals. So falsely do we see through the figurings of our dreading imagination, that without reasoning we should be lost. Reason can help us to see clearly, keep us from panic. If anyone wants to see how More saw clearly, he has but to read the "Dialogue of Comfort Against Tribulation." As all things in the Divine Comedy of Dante are mercilessly clear, so are they here.

There are three kinds of tribulation, says the wise and aged Hungarian Anthony. The first two kinds are medicinal, for one comes as a direct consequence of a particular sin, and warns us from, and punishes us for it; the other comes as a punishment for sins in general, and for the prevention of future sins. The third kind of tribulation is not medicinal; it is better than medicinal. It is given to a man for the exercise of his patience, and for the increase of his merit. More did not think he was above the need of the second kind of tribulation, but also he spoke of the third kind of tribulation in a humble yet intimate way which shows that he thought God might be offering him even the third kind of honoring tribulation. Anthony describes to his cousin Vincent how it is possible that a man might be guilty of a sin like manslaughter or adultery, but on being offered pardon at the price of renouncing his faith in Christ might by refusing to take that pardon, turn the tribulation of his execution into a source of merit. More was thinking of what honor martyrdom might bring him, a sinner, even though he was too much a sinner to deserve to be a martyr.

Tribulations can be divided into three kinds also, according to the way we receive them. There are some that come at our own wish, or which we inflict willingly on ourselves, for our soul's good. There are others sent by God, but which we accept gladly. The third kind we accept because we cannot put them from us. More, who saw everything from a practical point of view, gave his attention to the second kind of tribulation. He was not holy enough to have inflicted great voluntary tribulations on himself. He was not so unmindful of God's Providence to consider his tribulations as not to be rejoiced in. As he wrote to Meg, he had prayed for many things but never to be released from prison, nor to be delivered from the danger of death.

He reviewed in these dialogues conducted by Hungarians, all the ups and downs of his own life, not naming them as his own, but referring to the fame and to the worldly eminence such as had once been his, referring also to and mocking at the pardonable affection of his for his house at Chelsea. And then what great dangers there are in fame! It deceives so. — And More, the humanist knew what fame seems. — "But now to speak of the thing itself in his own proper nature, what is it but a blast of another man's mouth, as soon passed as spoken? And yet are there some fools so fed with this fond fantasy of fame, that they rejoice and glory to think, how they be continually praised all about, as though all the world did nothing else day and night, but ever sit and sing, *sanctus, sanctus, sanctus,* upon them."

And prosperity of which he had had a not mean
show? How difficult it was, he remembered, to
pray in prosperity! "But when men are wealthy
and well at their ease, while our tongue pattereth
upon our prayers apace, good God how many mad
ways our mind wandereth the while."

In high place as Chancellor, More had not
been wholly at ease. What he had practised there
to counteract the false sense of security and importance was probably what now Anthony in this
dialogue recommended. "Let him," counsels Anthony, speaking of the man in danger of becoming
proud, "Let him also choose himself some secret
solitary place in his own house, as far from noise
and company as he conveniently can, and thither
let him some time secretly resort alone, imagining
himself as one going out of the world even straight
unto the giving up his reckoning unto God of his
sinful living. Then let him there before an altar
or some pitiful image of Christ's bitter passion
(the beholding whereof may put him in remembrance of the thing, and move him to devout compassion) kneel down or fall prostrate as at the feet
of almighty God, verily believing him to be there
invisibly present as without any doubt he is. There
let him open his heart to God, and confess his
faults such as he can call to mind, and pray God
of forgiveness. Let him call to remembrance the
benefits that God hath given him, either in general

among other men, or privately to himself, and give him humble hearty thanks therefor. There let him declare unto God the temptations of the Devil, the suggestions of the flesh, the occasions of the world, and of his worldly friends, much worse many times in drawing a man from God, than are his most mortal enemies, which thing Our Saviour witnesseth himself, where he saith, Inimici hominis domestici eius: The enemies of a man are they that are his own familiars."

His own familiars! It was they who in this imprisonment of his tempted him the most, for he could easily leave his house which would soon forget him, or the comforts of a life in noble station, which were after all, he said, no great commodity. But his wife and his daughter when they came to see him really tempted him. While they stayed with him they made him feel singular in abstaining from the oath, — a thing which he hated to feel. — And when they left him, how much more silent and cold became his solitude. They both of them urged him to take the oath, and his Meg's voice was like the voice of his heart.

It was Cromwell himself who tolerated and connived at these visits. He knew how tempting they would be. And More himself knew how tempting they would be. And More himself knew how tempting they were. Often his wife is referred to as a "shrew," as if the word shrew had the

meaning then that it has now. It is taken for
granted because her husband twitted her on taking
more pains with her tight-lacing and pretty gir-
dles to arrive at perdition than saints did to arrive
at paradise, that he was willing to be well-rid of
her. They who so think do not understand the
freedom of More's banter, and they condemn a
wife whom biographers have found it too easy
to liken pedantically to Xantippe. More's second
wife had excellent household sense, and her husband appreciated it. "What the good-year!" quoth
that wife of his visiting the Tower. "I marvel
that you that have been always hitherto taken
for a wise man, will now so play the fool to lie
here in this close filthy prison, and be content
thus to be shut up among mice and rats, when
you might be abroad at your liberty, and with
the favor and good will both of the King and his
Council if you would but do as all the bishops and
best learned of this realm have done. And seeing
you have at Chelsea a right fair house, your
library, your gallery, your garden, your orchard,
and all other necessaries so handsome about you,
where you might in the company of me your wife,
your children, and household, be merry, I muse
what a God's name you mean here still thus
fondly to tarry."

More answered such raillery with a smile. Some
of the solicitude of his wife which showed her

good heart he did not answer at all. It touched him. For instance she could not understand how he could sleep with his door locked. He would suffocate, she thought. He started to remind her of the household truth that he was always having to bar doors and windows at home to keep that very same air out, that now for him she wanted in. He started to remind her of this, but caught himself.

He respected his wife's intentions, and her household wisdom, but she was not such an intelligence as could judge what the oath meant, or sway his own thoughts. With his daughter Meg, it was different. She was dear to his heart, but to his mind too she was akin, and respected companion. You might have thought from sheer affection or admiration for her father she would have taken the same stand as he. But no. She took a stand ever so near him, but not quite with him. All the friends who had praised him as a model of wisdom, now treated him as if he were doing something unwise. John Rastell, his brother-in-law, had been one of More's intimate circle. Merchant-adventurer, writer, playwright, he had been in some ways a kindred spirit. He had joined More in writing in defence of the doctrine of Purgatory. But now he had utterly changed. He had taken up with the doctrines of Tyndale, and was raging against the monastic orders and their wealth, wishing to suppress some of them for their laxity, but most of all the Carthusians because they were too austere. Others of More's friends had not so fantastically left him. Tunstall, for instance, was only for submission to the king, but Tunstall was so near to him in love of wit and learning, and had inspired More with such respect, that to be deserted by him caused a deep pang. As for Erasmus, it went without saying what he would think. And finally to persuade him to join the multitude of his apparently righteous friends, he had this daughter of his with her loving letters, winning affection, and most fervent solicitude. Was ever mortal tempted by such an Eve.

More did not answer his daughter with mere banter. He laid open to her how he had not taken his stand lightly:

"I forgot not in this matter the counsel of Christ in the Gospel, that ere I should begin to build this castle for the safeguard of mine own soul, I should sit and reckon what the charge would be. I counted, Marget, full surely many a restless night, while my wife slept, and weened I had slept too, what peril were possible for to fall to me, so far forth that I am sure there can come none above. And in devising, daughter, thereupon, I had a full heavy heart. But yet I thank Our Lord for all that, I never thought to change, though the very uttermost should hap me that my fear ran upon."

Meg begged him to change his mind before it was too late. "Too late, daughter," he exclaimed. "I beseech Our Lord, that if ever I make such a change it may be too late indeed. For well I wot the change cannot be good for my soul, that change I say that should grow but by fear."

More told her that should the King be able to look in his conscience as God did, the King would never ask him to take the oath. But the King could not see into his conscience, and neither could Meg, for even Meg by More was not allowed to see all of his reasoning. He had, he said, some secret reasons, which he did not wish to divulge. She must trust him because she knew him.

The word secret applied by More to some of his undivulged reasonings has led some to think that he had mysterious reasons, or owned scandalous information relative to the morals of Anne Boleyn or of Anne Boleyn's sister, which are secret in the sense of being such as too-knowing people like to spread about in a low voice. That is not, I believe, More's meaning when he says that some of his reasons are secret. He means, to begin with, that they are reasons which are nobody else's affair, which are nevertheless truly his. They are opinions of his come to him by his intuition, and by his sane practical foresight, the acceptance of which, he thinks he has no right to force on others. What these opinions were we can only di-

vine by regarding some other opinions of his which
he mentioned not directly in this affair of the oath.

More had resigned from the Chancellorship
when the clergy made their famous first act of submission to the royal power. That he considered
that act as direfully important is indicated in many
ways: first, by the very fact of his resignation;
then by the scathing remark of his that the bishops
— whom he kept himself from reproving, — had
shown themselves ignorant of the doctrines appertaining to their holy religion. It was not, that
the man Henry had replaced the man Warham,
or the man Cranmer. It was that the Temporalty
was being put in the wrong place; the Spiritualty
was being debased in a manner not only unpleas-
ing to God, but fraught with consequences which
he trembled at as destructive to civilization, but
which all save he and the "blind" bishop —
so-called — of Rochester, Fisher, refused to take
notice of. The bishops, according to Chapuys,
Ambassador of Charles V, were by their act of
submission set in a lower position than the cob-
blers, who could for their own organization make
regulations. — They were, indeed. — And what
More, who loved true order, saw as a result of
this wrenching of the rightful organization of
things, was the spread of heresy, which otherwise
might have been checked, but which now he was
ready, contrary to the opinion of the King and his

friends, to see as very soon in England triumphing. Catholics he prophesied would find themselves lucky in the near future to have anywhere in the island where they could worship. And the changing of the English Church into something merely national would lead to the breaking up of that unified Christendom, which was held together by the Universal Spirituality. Once the spiritual unity was gone, all that could be expected would be wars and more wars: division and division.

More was aghast at this Act of Supremacy because, as a father sees that a son is running toward destruction, as a weatherwise sailor foresees a storm, he saw the England in its despair that was to be; with its hundred sects, its misbeliefs, its mystifications. He saw the Europe, disunited, and nationalized that we know. He had some inkling of our class-wars, our world-war. But these flashes of clairvoyance, granted to him because of his truth-filled head, which was illumined with that Spirit which can illumine truth and truth only, these matters so evident to his penetrating eyes, but so dark to so many others, how could he expect his daughter, even though she were his second self, to see them as he saw them? So he kept them secret from her. They were not matters of faith. They were not the essential thing. He preferred to be not a teacher to Meg, but her companion.

And most of all he did not wish to present himself to her or to anyone else as their superior in courage. He was firm and in his firmness begged that they desist from trying to change him, as he desisted from trying to change them, but otherwise, he was dependent on them. Let Meg try to help him, (who was not a hero), praying that he might not go back on his conscience, and listening to him when he acknowledged that he sometimes felt faint, which was, he said, a good thing, for it taught both of them to put all their trust in God. "Mistrust Him," he said of God to Meg, "will I not, though I feel me faint. Yea, and though I should feel my fear even at point to overthrow me too, yet shall I remember how Saint Peter with a blast of wind began to sink for his faint faith, and shall do as he did, call upon Christ and pray Him to help."

And they always parted, the father merry, stronger than the daughter. And sometimes too the daughter was merry and could laugh at herself and her importunity. She acknowledged once that among those who complained of her father's obstinacy was Henry Pattensen, More's professional fool, now employed by the Lord Mayor of London. "What," said the fool, "Has Sir Thomas refused the oath? Why should he refuse? Have not I taken it?"

Winter passed. The King had his winter pag-

eants. The Spring came. On the last day of April
Cromwell came to visit More. Had not More
seen, he asked, the new statutes which Parliament had enacted? — New statutes indeed! —
In November Parliament had enacted: "Albeit
the King's Majesty justly and rightfully is, and
ought to be, supreme head of the Church of England, and so is recognized by the clergy of this
realm in their convocations; yet nevertheless, for
corroboration and confirmation thereof, and for
increase of virtue in Christ's religion within this
realm of England, and to repress and extirpate
all errors, heresies, and other enormities and abuses
heretofore used in the same, be it enacted, by the
authority of this present parliament, that the
King, our sovereign lord, his heirs, and successors, kings of this realm, shall be taken, accepted
and reputed, the only supreme head in earth of
the Church of England, called Anglicana Ecclesia and shall have and enjoy, annexed and
united to the imperial crown of this realm, as well
the title and style thereof as all honours, dig-
nities, immunities, profits, and commodities to
the said dignity of supreme head of the said
Church belonging and appertaining."

And the Act went on with its hypocrisy, pretense and innovation, and was followed by another
act dealing punishment to all who did not bow
down to that Act and worship it. It declared it

high treason for anybody after the first day of
February "maliciously to wish, will or devise by
words or writing, or by craft imagine, invent,
practise, or attempt any bodily harm to be done
or committed to the king's most royal person,
the queen's, or their heirs apparent, or deprive
them or any of them of their dignity, title or name
or their royal estates, or slanderously and maliciously publish and pronounce, by express writing
or words, that the king our sovereign lord, should
be heretic, schismatic, infidel" — that is things
which evidently an honest man saw he would be
called. — And so on.

Had More seen these acts? He had. Then would
he kindly give his opinion about the Supremacy;
that is, incriminate himself or submit. "Where-
unto I answered" said More, "that in good faith
I had well trusted, that the King's highness
would never have commanded any such question
to be demanded of me, considering that I ever
from the beginning, well and truly from time
to time declared my mind unto his highness;
and since that time (I said) unto your Master-
ship, Master Secretary, also, by mouth and by
writing. And now I have in good faith discharged
my mind of all such matters, and neither will
dispute King's titles nor pope's: but the King's
true faithful subject I am, and will be, and daily
I pray for him, and all his, and for you all that

are of his honourable council, and for all the realm. And otherwise than this, I never intend to meddle."

Cromwell explained to him what a generous sovereign he had, inclining not so much to rigor as to mercy. The King would be so glad to see More in the world again. More answered that not for the whole world would he meddle with the world again, that his whole study was upon the Passion of Christ, and his passage out of this world. Cromwell left him.

The news of this interview with all the forebodings it suggested, was sent by More in a letter to Margaret Roper. She saw what More had foreseen all along, that it was now not merely a question of imprisonment. It was a question of putting to death. She begged therefore to be allowed to see her father.

On May fourth she was so allowed. It was a day especially selected, for it was the day of a pageant: the pageant of the terror of death to be presented by Thomas Cromwell the one playwright, to Thomas More the other playwright, on such a stage as could be seen from his prison window. More and his daughter looked out into the Spring weather. Blessed John Houghton, Blessed Augustine Webster, Blessed Robert Lawrence, — Carthusian priors all, — and Blessed Richard Reynolds, Brigittine monk, lover of God, and great pursuer of learning, and Blessed John Hale, vicar of Isleworth, were emerging from the Tower to be fixed to their hurdles and dragged to Tyburn, there to die the death of traitors, because they refused to acknowledge the Supremacy of the King over the Church; there to die the death of traitors which was certainly very precious by its pain, for it was a manner of dying in which you were eviscerated by an adroit knife before you were properly hanged, and after a view of your entrails were cut into four pieces for the view of others.

"Lo, dost thou not see, Meg," said More to his daughter, as they watched these merry men going to their execution, "Lo, dost thou not see, that these blessed fathers be now as cheerfully going to their deaths as bridegrooms to their marriage? Wherefore, thereby mayest thou see, mine own good daughter, what a great difference there is between such as have in effect spent all their days in a strait and penitential and painful life religiously, and such as have in the world, like worldly wretches (as thy poor father hath done), consumed all their time in pleasure and ease licentiously. For God, considering their long-continued life in most sore and grievous penance, will no longer suffer them to remain here in this vale of misery, but speedily hence taketh them to the fruition of His everlasting Deity. Whereas

thy silly father, Meg, that like a wicked caitiff
hath passed forth the whole course of his miserable life most sinfully, God, thinking him not
worthy so soon to come to that eternal felicity,
leaveth him here still in this world further to be
plagued and turmoiled with misery."

"The pinch is in the pain." So said the two
Hungarians talking together about persecution.
So said the younger of them, Vincent, fearing
the bloody persecution of the Turks. So acknowledged the elder of the twain, sagacious Anthony.
What does imprisonment do but rid us of some
very doubtful commodities? And how little different is prison life from life out of prison, for
life itself is a prison, where we are all doomed
sooner or later to be executed and where we are
all straitened, and corrected? But even though
some of the pain due to our body may be figment
of imagination, yet foolish would he be who be-
littled bodily pain. Death is a thing terrible. A
thought can not put an end to its terror. The
consolation of the noble but pagan philosophers
can not assuage it.

Cromwell who was later to be panic-stricken
at his own death, crying "Mercy, Mercy, Mercy,"
was busy awakening all dreads of death he could
in More, and in all who felt like More. He was
busy persecuting another rank of the Carthusians,
who, he hoped, might not be as steadfast as the

first. They were Humphrey Middlemore, William Exmew, and Sebastian Newdigate, the last of whom had been a courtier and an intimate of the King, and all three of whom are thus spoken of by the old chronicler: "These were gentlemen." And like gentlemen they were treated. They were imprisoned first in the Tower of London, where they remained seventeen days, "standing" says that same chronicler "both upright, tied with iron collars fast by the necks to the posts of the prison, and great fetters fast rived on their legs with great iron bolts; straitly tied that they could neither lie nor sit, nor otherwise ease themselves, but stand upright, and in all that space were they never losed for any natural necessity, nor voyding of ordure or otherwise. And they could get no meat but bread alone, and flesh, which in no wise they would eat, being contrary to their Rule and profession."

On the second of June these Carthusians and the so-called "blind bishop," Fisher, who had been by the Pope created Cardinal while in the Tower, were indicted for treason. They were all found — if found is the right word — guilty, and were put to death during June: the Carthusians on the nineteenth, Cardinal Fisher — by a less severe death on the Tower Hill from an axe — on the longest day of the year, the twenty-second.

There is something heroical about these deaths

to us. They are inspiriting. Think of emaciated
Fisher being waked up on his day of execution a
little too early, and asking to be allowed to sleep
an hour or two longer; and then of his speech
at his execution. "When this bishop, with his
deadly carcass, stood up thus on the scaffold,
then spake he to the people in effect: 'Christian
people, I am come hither to die for the faith of
Christ's Catholic Church. And, I thank God,
hitherto my stomach hath served me well therto,
so that yet hitherto I have not feared death.
Wherefore I desire you help me, and assist me
with your prayers, that at the very point and
instant of my death's stroke, and in the very
moment of my death, I then faint not in any point
of the Catholic faith for any fear. And I pray God
save the King, and the realm, and hold his holy
hand over it, and send the King a good counsel."

More did not hear such speeches, nor know the
anecdotes we know. He merely knew that death
was taking others as it approached him. And doors
of escape from it were always being left open to
him. Dr. Wilson, who on that day at Lambeth
had been as brave as More himself, had given
in. This was made known to More. And rumors
were spread that More had given in, so that he
could receive letters, as he did, in congratulation
on his return to sense. And time and time again
the members of the Council argued with him.

For the most part their arguments were suggestions to his imagination: let him give in, and be loved by the King once more, and laugh in the world. But one question of Cromwell's gave him an opportunity to define his position, for the question was a subtle one, probably a suggestion of Cranmer who was also present. The question was this: why did More examine heretics and demand of them whether or not they believed the Pope to be head of the Church — for which thing Cromwell praised him — if he was now unwilling to let them demand of him whether he did or did not think the King was head of the Church. More said he did not care to defend himself, but he pointed out that a law of all Christendom — which established the Pope as head of the Church, — was a quite different thing from a merely local law of England.

Arguments were at an end. The pageant of the terror of death had been played before More's eyes, and in vain. Now More had but to be inflicted with death, which infliction required first an indictment, which was a thing that against More, the lawyer, had carefully to be attended to. A man named Rich, newly named the King's solicitor, and duly trained by past experience for dishonesty, came to the Tower, bringing with him two men, his accomplices but with still a tinge of conscience: Sir Richard Southwell, and

Master Palmer, servant to Cromwell. Their
errand was to deprive More of his books and
writing materials; a punishment meted to him
with a show of justice for it had been proved that
he had carried on a perfectly harmless, but duly
secret correspondence with his fellow-prisoner in
the Tower, Fisher. And the three had another
errand which was more important and which
could hide itself behind the other: get More to
speak indiscreetly, unguardedly, some of his
opinions. Listen to him while you pack the books.

So while the other two, Palmer and Southwell,
were packing the books, Rich was in conversation with the astute More. He asked More if
More would not accept him, Rich, as King if
Parliament should so decree.

"Yes, Sir," quote Sir Thomas More. "That
would I." Then Rich asked him another question,
still as in idle conversation. If Parliament should
elect him, — Rich, — Pope, would not More accept him as Pope?"

More answered such a question with a better
question: "Suppose the Parliament would make a
law that God should not be God; would you then,
Master Rich, say that God were not God?"

One thing was certain: More somehow was going to be indicted, and More knew it, and foresaw
the torment of his consequent execution. He
strengthened himself as Anthony advised Vincent

to strengthen himself by contrasting that torment with Hell's torment; and then by, even better, contrasting it with his Christian picture of heaven: "the great glory of God, the Trinity in this High Marvellous Majesty, our Saviour in his glorious manhead sitting on his throne, with this immaculate mother and all that glorious company, calling us there unto them." No man who sees such a sight, could shrink from death.

Chapter XII

EXECUTION

"Thomas Palmer, miles; Thomas Spert, miles; Gregorius Lovell, armiger; Thomas Burbage, armiger; Willielmus Brown, armiger; Jasper Leyke, armiger; Thomas Byllington, armiger; Johannes Parnell, gent'; Galfridus Chamber, gent'; Edward Stokwod, gent'; Ricardus Bellamy, gent'; Georgius Stokys, gent'." These are the names of the jurymen whom on July 1st, 1535, More had been called to face. They were his neighbors, for they lived near the Tower, in which he was accused of having committed treason. They were his peers. They were Englishmen. They were England.

His judges — let us say they represented not England, but the King — were Lord Audley, the Lord Chancellor; Thomas, Duke of Norfolk; Charles, Duke of Suffolk; the Earl of Huntingdon; the Earl of Cumberland; the Earl of Wiltshire, (father to Anne Boleyn); Lord Montague; Lord Rochford, (brother of Anne Boleyn); Lord Windsor; Thomas Cromwell, secretary; Sir John Fitz-James, chief justice of the King's bench; Sir John Baldwin, chief justice of the common pleas;

Sir Richard Lister, chief baron of the exchequer; Sir William Paulet; Sir John Porte; Sir John Spellman; Sir Walter Luke; Sir William Fitz-William; Sir Anthony Fitz-Herbert. These men were justices of the King's bench. They had summoned Thomas More to appear before them, and inasmuch as they were not wilful murderers, — and yet were to commit murder — and were at worst drawn by avarice, or by ambition like the two Boeyns, or by a twisted sense of loyalty to their King, we can say of them, generously, that they did not see this very Thomas More whom they had summoned. They saw instead a man who had turned obstinate and singular, an intellectual who persisted in using his mind on subjects concerning which he had no obligation to think: a bothersome misguided somebody, an eccentric, different from themselves. They did not desire, directly, to be cruel to him, but they had to be rid of him.

Listen to the indictment. It was six pages long, written in Latin, prolix as if with veracity, filled with legal repetitions as if to appear more legal. That parliament, which had met in 1529, and which had not yet been dissolved, had on November third of the preceding autumn, in the twenty-sixth year of King Henry's reign, enacted that the King was unique and supreme head on earth of the Church in England. It had also enacted that any man who maliciously by word or deed tried to deprive the King and his heirs of that rightful title was guilty of treason, and should receive the punishment for treason. Sir Thomas More, lodging in the Tower, had "turned his eyes from God," and allowing himself to be "seduced by the Devil," committed that very crime of treason, and was deserving of that punishment which treason deserves.

In what way he had offended was then recorded. He had in the Tower of London, on May 1st, on its seventh day, before Sir Thomas Cromwell, and a cleric, Thomas Bedyll, and a doctor of laws, John Tregonell, refused to assent to or to dissent from the above Act of Supremacy; showing thereby a malicious desire to overturn the King; and answering only in the English words — remember the indictment was otherwise in Latin — "I will not meddle with any such matters, for I am fully determined to serve God, and to think upon his passion and my passage out of this world."

Furthermore this traitor to his King had conspired with a clergyman, John Fisher, then also for misprision of treason held in the Tower, and had encouraged that Fisher in his obstinacy, which was proved by the fact that letters were known to have passed between them, and by the similarity of the responses Fisher and More had given

before their examiners. Both these men had spoken
of a two-edged sword, saying that the present statute was like that instrument. Fisher before the
King's commissioners had said: "I will not meddle
with that matter, for the statute is like a two-
edged sword. And, if I should answer one way,
I should offend my conscience; and if I should
answer the other way I should put my life in
jeopardy, wherefore I will make no answer to
that matter." And More's words later on before
the commissioners had been similar: "The law
and statute whereby the King is made supreme
head, as is aforesaid, be like a sword with two
edges; for if a man say that the same laws be good,
then it is dangerous to the soul; and if he say contrary to the said statute, then it is death to the
body. Wherefore I will make thereunto none other
answer because I will not be occasion of the short-
ing of my life." Both these answers were but
echoes of what More himself had said in a letter
to Fisher. More was responsible for his own
treason, and for Fisher's.

Finally on June twelfth, — which was but a
little over two weeks previous to his trial — More
before Richard Rich had used words which showed
his malicious mind. Rich had talked about "What
if I should be elected King by Parliament?" or
"What if I should be elected Pope?" And More
had answered: "What if Parliament should declare

that God was not God?" And then More had unguardedly let drop the fatal words, that Parliament had no power to make Henry head of the Church, and that even if he should be taken for such in England, in the rest of Christendom he would not be so taken.

Scarcely was the terrible indictment read, itself so malicious, and threatening death, than the Duke of Norfolk and the Lord Chancellor broke in with their now so familiar offer of pardon: "Sir Thomas More, ye see that ye have heinously offended the King's Majesty; howbeit we are in very good hope (such is his great bounty, benignity and clemency) that if you will revoke and reform your wilful, obstinate opinion that you have so wrongfully maintained and so long dwelt in, that ye shall taste of his gratious pardon."

"My Lords," quote Sir Thomas More, "I do most humbly thank your Honours of your great good will towards me. Howbeit, I make this my boon and petition unto God as heartily as I may, that he will vouchsafe this my good, honest and upright mind to nourish, maintain and uphold in me even to the last hour, and extreme moment that ever I shall live.

"Concerning now the matters you charge and challenge me withall, the articles are so prolix and long that I fear, what for my long imprisonment, what for my long lingering disease, what

for my present weakness and debility, that neither
my wit, nor my memory, not yet my voice, will
serve to make so full, so effectual and sufficient
answer as the weight and importance of these
matters crave."

He was no longer the young More he had been.
He was no longer the comely Chancellor who for
all the pain in his chest, could nevertheless cheerfully about the court present a picture of moderate
health. His beard gave him an appearance un-
trim, and he was unsteady with fatigue. To listen
to such a long indictment after fifteen months
of imprisonment, and to listen to it standing,
must have made him dizzy. He was leaning on a
staff. They brought him a chair. He sat down,
and began his defence, — his legal defence.

In the first place in regard to his silence when
presented with the Statute of Supremacy: how
could he incur danger by that silence? "Neither
your law," he said, "nor any law in the world
is able justly and rightly to punish me, unless
you may besides lay to my charge either some
word or some fact in deed."

At this time the King's attorney broke in that
the silence showed a "repining against the statute"; to which More's cool legal answer was that
in civil law silence implies rather confirmation
than condemnation.

Then More defended himself from the charge

of having encouraged Fisher to his disobedience.
Yes, he had written letters to Fisher. They were
from a legal point of view quite harmless. If he
had used the phrase "two-edged sword," it had
been in connection with imaginary cases of conscience; he had never applied it directly to the
statute. He had never told Fisher what to do.
And firmly he finished up: "These are the tenours
of my letters, upon which you can take no hold
or handfast by your law to condemn me to death."

After this Rich entered in. He was the man
who had been sent to the Tower to lure More into
unguarded conversation. He was chosen to be
sent because it was known that even if he did not
succeed in making More speak what he should not
speak, he was enough of a liar to pretend that he
had. It was trusted confidently that he had no
fear of perjury and would at this trial, in spite
of his oath to speak the truth, speak all the necessary lies, for which in the due course of time, he
was to be knighted. Rich repeated what had been
said in the indictment: More had verbally denied
the King's supremacy over the Church.

Everyone knew Rich was a liar, and More knew
they knew it. His savage response to Rich's evidence was not a sign that he had lost control of
himself, but a manner of discrediting the sole
witness against him.

"If I were a man" — the accent was very ironically upon the *I* — "If I were a man," began the defendant, "that did not regard an oath, I needed not, as it is well known, in this place, at this time, nor in this case, to stand here as an accused person. And if this oath of yours, Master Rich, be true, then pray I that I never see God in the face, which I would not say, were it otherwise, to win the whole world."

More had known Rich all his life, and now he was looking at Rich: "And I, as you know, of no small while have been acquainted with you and your conversation, who have known you from your youth hitherto; for we long dwelled in one parish together, where, as your self can well tell (I am sorry you compell me so to say) you were esteemed very light of tongue, a common liar, a great dicer, and of no commendable fame. And so in your house at the Temple, where hath been your chief bringing up, were you likewise accompted."

Which of these two men, More or Rich, were these jurymen, representing England, going to believe?

And besides that, how could anyone think it was likely that he who had such contempt for Rich, would in so grave a case trust the secrets of his conscience to such a man, when he refused to the King's commissioners those same secrets? He had conversed with Rich, but he had never spoken his mind of the King's Supremacy. Call

in the other witnesses. Enter Southwell and
Palmer. They said they had been so busy trussing
up the books which they were taking away from
More's cell that they had not tried to follow the
conversation between More and Rich.

Would the jury still believe Rich?

And suppose More had spoken unguardedly
about the Statute of Supremacy, would that, he
asked, make him guilty of having spoken maliciously? In that very act of Parliament by which he
was indicted, those guilty of treason had to do
more than speak against the King's claims, they
had to speak or work maliciously against them.
Maliciously had been carefully and deliberately
included in the statute at the insistence of the
House of Lords, for it had been seen that life
would be intolerable if every idle word might
endanger a man's head, and prove temptation to
an eavesdropper. And how could Thomas More
be held to have spoken maliciously to Richard
Rich? Yes, acknowledged More, if "malitia be
taken generally for sin, no man is there then that
thereof can excuse himself," but it is not. It
means in the context not "malitia" in the general
sense, but "malevollentia," or "malevolence," and
it is as material a part of the statute as the word
"forcible" is in the statute of "forcible entry,"
which distinguishes that kind of entry from
"peaceable entry."

So far More had treated the court as if it were what it pretended to be, a court of law. He had taken none but legal considerations into account. He had proved himself "not guilty"; he had not tried to prove himself a martyr.

The jury retired, was absent fifteen minutes, came back with the verdict (dictated by intimidation) "guilty."

Up stood the Lord Chancellor to pronounce judgment, but More — still the lawyer, — knowing better than any there the law, interrupted him:

"My Lord, when I was toward the law, the manner in such case was to ask the prisoner, before judgment, why judgment should not be given against him."

More was allowed to speak and he called in question not the indictment now, but the Act of Parliament upon which the indictment was grounded. It was not valid. It was contrary to the constitution of Christendom. No temporal prince may by any law take upon himself a spiritual preëminence which rightfully belongs to the See of Rome, and which was granted by the mouth of Our Saviour himself to St. Peter, and to his successors. England might no more pass that Act of Supremacy against the general law of Christ's universal Catholic Church, "no more than the City of London" — these are More's own words — "being but one poor member in respect of the whole realm, might make a law against an Act of Parliament to bind the whole realm."

Not only was the law against the laws of Christendom. It was contrary to the laws of England, to the still unrepealed Magna Carta: "Quod ecclesia Anglicana libera sit, et habeat omnia iura sua integra, et libertates suas illaesas." It was also contrary to the "sacred oath which the King's highness himself and every Christian prince always with great solemnity received at their coronations." And he went further, alleging "that no more might this realm of England refuse obedience to the See of Rome than might the child refuse obedience to his natural father."

Once the Chancellor interrupted More's eloquence. Weakly he remonstrated what had been said so many times that it had grown ever feebler than when it first sounded: "Think of all the learned men of this realm, the bishops, the universities, which have consented to this act." You are alone. But the remonstance only drew more strongly what More had hitherto pronounced with reserve: he was with Christendom. He was with the dead: "The now holy saints in heaven." And he ended the rejoinder thus: "And therefore am I not bounden, my Lord, to conform my conscience to the Council of one realm against the general council of Christendom. For of the aforesaid holy bishops I have, for every bishop of yours, above one hundred; and for one council or parliament of yours (God knoweth what manner of one), I have all the councils made these thousand years. And for this one kingdom, I have all the Christian realm."

Broke in at this the Duke of Norfolk, thinking to score a point: "We now plainly perceive that ye are maliciously bent."

"Nay, nay," quoth Sir Thomas More, "very and pure necessity, for the discharge of my conscience, enforceth me to speak so much. Wherein I call and appeal to God whose only sight pierceth into the very depth of man's heart, to be my witness. Howbeit, it is not for this supremacy so much that ye seek my blood, as for that I would not condescend to the marriage."

The flurry of repartee was now over, and the Lord Chancellor put his head together with that of the Chief Justice, Sir John Fitz-James. How about this invalidity of the statute? Was there legal significance in anything Sir Thomas had said about the general law of Christendom? And if there was could judgment be pronounced? There was a real fear of More the lawyer. The Chief Justice replied bluffly as if he settled something: "My Lords all, by Saint Julian, I must needs confess that, if the Act of Parliament be lawful, then the indictment is good enough."

So the indictment was considered good enough. Judgment was forthwith pronounced. Sir Thomas was condemned to be hanged, drawn and quartered. Had the condemned anything to say?

The lawyer More had had his say, first the lawyer who knew the laws of England, then the lawyer who knew the justice of Christendom. Now spoke the martyr, — seeing he must be a martyr. Noblesse oblige. There were his words: "More have I not to say, my Lords, but that like as the blessed Apostle Saint Paul, as we read in the Acts of the Apostles, was present and consented to the death of Saint Stephen, and kept their clothes that stoned him to death, and yet be they now both twain holy saints in heaven, and shall continue there friends together forever, so I verily trust, and shall therefore rightly pray, that though your Lordships have now here in earth been judges to my condemnation, we may yet hereafter in heaven merrily all meet together, to our everlasting salvation. And thus I desire Almighty God to preserve and defend the King's Majesty, and to send him good counsel."

— What exquisite courtesy to liken his judges to St. Paul! —

He was led to the Tower then by Sir William Kingston, making a picture of the King's vengeance before the eyes of the townspeople, for an axe was carried before him with its edge turned towards him, a sign of condemnation.

The first interruption in the journey came from

More's only son, John, who cast himself at his father's feet, not without tears craving his father's blessing, and being by him blessed and kissed most lovingly.

Sir Thomas More did not weep.

And then as they came to the place called the Old Swan, which was, we are told, in sight of Saint Anthony's school, where under grammarian Holt, More at seven years had begun his letters, Sir William Kingston, his conductor, a strong, tall and comely knight, known for his stoical if not cruel heart, bade good-bye to him, and as he bade good-bye showed the tears on his cheek. "Good Mr. Kingston," said More, "trouble not yourself, but be of good cheer, for I will pray for you and my good lady your wife, that we may meet in heaven together, where we shall be merry for ever and ever."

More went on still with dry eyes, not with a face of stone, but with a face of every day; and as they came to the Tower Wharf, Meg rushed in among the halberts, and threw her arms about his neck, not being able to say any words but "O my father! O my father!" Scarcely had she been torn from him, scarcely had he gone some ten steps farther, than Meg completely forgetful of herself, of her surroundings, and only ravished by the love of her father, dashed in again through the escort, threw her arms about him once more, kissed him and kissed him; drawing from him this time no words, but only a shining tear. And all the troop were in tears. And Margaret Giggs embraced him. And Dorothy Collie, the maid-servant embraced him. And on they went.

The Tower again. After the strain of the trial More reposed himself, and resumed all those ways which were natural to him: his meditations, his jests; his reasonings, his mockings of the Devil. Is there really any difference between dying, one's head on a block under an axe, and dying, pining in bed? "Some we hear in their death bed complain, that they feel sharp knives cut in two their heart strings. Some cry out and think they feel within the brain-pan their head pricked even full of pins. And they that lie in a pleurisy think that every time they cough, they feel a sharp sword swap them to the heart."

And he thought again of the glory of the heaven. What if you did lose your head on your way to that glory? "Now to this great glory can there no man come headless. Our head is Christ: and therefore to Him must we be joined, and as members of His must we follow him, if we will come hither. He is our guide to guide us hither, and is entered in before us, and he therefore that will enter in after, the same way that Christ walked, the same way must he walk. And what was the way by which He walked into heaven? Himself showeth what way it was that His Father provided for him, where He said unto the two disciples going toward the castle of Emmaus: Knew you not that Christ must suffer passion, and by that way enter into his kingdom? Who can for very shame desire to enter into the kingdom of Christ with ease, when Himself entered not into His own without pain?"

More could be more care-free than ever with his jests. He was but a few days from Heaven, and could not take some of the important things of this life as important at all. A young courtier, sent by the King, came to More begging and importuning him, at this later hour, to change his mind, that is to submit to the King. More fatigued by the constant "change your mind, change your mind," did, to rid himself of the young popinjay, announce: "Well, my mind is changed."

And the young man ran to the King, and while More had forgotten even what he had said, repeated excitedly that More had changed his mind. "What mind?" asked the King and sent the blunderer back to find from More what mind had been changed. And More, whose sanctity and sanity was doubted by the Protestant-minded Chronicler Hall because in serious moments he made jests, wondered what in the world was the matter with the young fool: "For my meaning was," he said, "that whereas I had purposed to have been shaven, that I might seem to others as I before was wont; my mind is changed, for that I intend my beard shall take such part as my head doth."

More wrote at least two leave-taking letters from the Tower, one to Bonvisi, a very rich Italian merchant from Lucca, with whom he was more affectionately intimate than with any other even English merchant. And in justice to Bonvisi let it be said that he deserved it, for he sent wine and meat regularly every week to the Tower, and now that he knew More was to die, he sent him with a gala lavishness which not all London was destined to show, a suit of Camelot silk in which to die. More wrote to him in Latin, calling him half his heart and bewailing that he could never repay him for half his kindnesses, but reminding him that God for his mercy's sake "will bring us from this wretched and stormy world, into his rest, where shall need no letters, where no walls shall dissever us, where no porter shall keep us from talking together, but that we may have the fruition of the eternal joy with God the Father, and with his only begotten son Our Redeemer Jesus Christ, with the holy Spirit of them both, the Holy Ghost proceeding from them both."

But More's final letter was to his daughter. It was written the day before his execution. It is unique for its careful attendance to household things, and for its talk in the same breath of the highest joys of paradise.

"Our Lord bless you good daughter, and your good husband, and your little boy, and all yours, and all my children, and all my God-children, and all your friends. Recommend me when you may to my good daughter Cicely, whom I beseech Our Lord to comfort. And I send her my blessing, and to all her children, and I pray her to pray for me. I send her an handkercher: and God comfort my good son her husband. My good daughter Daunce hath the picture in parchment, that you delivered me from my Lady Coniers, the name is on the back side. Show her that I heartily pray her, that you may send it in my name to her again, for a token from me to pray for me. I like especially well Dorothy Collie, I pray you be good unto her. I would wit whether this be she you wrote me of. If not I pray you be good to the other, as you may in her affliction, and to my good daughter Joane Aleyn too. Give her, I pray you, some kind answer, for she sued hither to me this day to pray you be good to her.

"I cumber you good Margaret much, but I would be sorry if it should be any longer than tomorrow. For it is Saint Thomas's even, and the utas (octave) of Saint Peter: and therefore tomorrow long I to go to God: it were a day very mete and convenient to me.

"I never liked your manner toward me better, than when you kissed me last. For I love when

daughterly love and dear charity hath no leisure
to look to worldly courtesy.

"Farewell my dear child, and pray for me, and
I shall for you and all your friends, that we may
merrily meet in heaven. I thank you for your great
cost. I send now to my good daughter Clement her
algorism stone, and I send her and my godson and
all here God's blessing and mine. I pray you at
time convenient recommend me to my good son,
John More. I like well his natural fashion. Our Lord
bless him and his good wife my loving daughter, to
whom I pray him be good as he hath great cause:
and that if the land of mine come to his hand, he
break not my will concerning his sister Daunce.
And Our Lord bless Thomas and Austin and all
that they shall have."

"I like well his natural fashion." Had More said
of his son John. It was in "natural fashion" that
More the next day, the sixth of July, the octave of
St. Peter, went to execution.

Sir Thomas Pope, an old friend of More's, had
waked him his last day on earth and birthday in
Heaven. He had been sent to More by the King,
and he acquainted More with the fact that today
he was to die. More was all thanks to the messenger
who gave him good news, and to the King who had
given him such a seclusion in which to meditate on
death. But the King was even kinder than that. He
had pardoned More from being hanged, drawn, and

quartered. He was merely to be beheaded on
Tower Hill. "God keep my friends," said More,
"from the pardon of the King!" And the King was
to allow his daughter and wife at his burial. And
the King asked as a favor that More speak but few
words at his execution.

More put on the suit of camelot-silk which
Bonvisi had sent him, at which the Lieutenant of
the Tower remonstrated: the executioner, a mere
rascal would get the suit in fee. "Shall I account
him a rascal," exclaimed More, "that shall do me
this day so singular a benefit?" Yet he changed his
suit, open as always to good counsel, and not un-
thrifty where thrift was due, but asking Roper to
send the man a gold angel.

His last half hour of life was as natural as any
other hour of his. No dramatic appearance of
martyrdom did he put on to estrange himself from
the common run of his fellow-citizens, or to pretend
that he, citizen More, had suddenly turned hero in
romance and better than they.

Yet wonderful things happened. Among them,
a man from Winchester suffering from a temptation to despair and suicide accosted him on his way
to execution. More, who in his acquaintance with
the religious aberrations of his fellow-Londoners,
had come to know such temptations, and to pity
those obsessed by them, had been in years gone by
a help to the man. He had, indeed, brought peace

to his frayed mind. But since More had been imprisoned in the Tower, the temptations had again
harassed the poor victim, and now in agony he
called on More, whose temptations were so different from his, for help. "Go and pray for me," said
Sir Thomas More, "and I will carefully pray for
you." And the man from then on had peace of
mind.

More in his last moments befriended all those
near him with his jests. The ladder leading to the
scaffold was rickety, and More who had leaned on
a staff at his trial, had now need of the Lieutenant's
hand. "I pray thee see me safe up, and for my
coming down let me shift for myself."

Pride of martyrdom was not there, but neither
was indifference. In his few words to the people he
asked them to pray for him, and to bear witness
with him that he should here suffer death in and
for the Catholic Church. And his very last words
were even more precise, and yet in spite of their
absolute quietness and sobriety clear even to our
own day. "I die loyal to God and the King, but to
God first of all."

His lips moved in a short prayer as he kneeled on
the scaffold: — the Miserere. Then with the lips
which had said the prayer and which then had
kissed the executioner, he to the executioner made
merry. "Pluck up thy spirit, man, and be not
afraid to do thy office; my neck is very short; take

heed therefore that thou strike not awry, for saving
of thy honesty."

Then he covered his own eyes, saying to the
executioner who had tried to do it for him: "Nay,
I will cover them myself." His eyes, which were so
much his, would be blinded by no other.

He stretched himself full length on the scaffold,
for it was necessary so to do, the execution-block
being no more than a low log. Measured thus at
full humility he made but a second's delay in order
to shove the beard, which he was not used to, out
over the block, at the same time remarking that it
was not to be cut: "it had never committed
treason."

Then the axe descended severing so appropriately that part of him which was so guilty in a
great confusion and perplexity of having thought
straight: his head.